BRITAIN IN CH

1

Colin McNab
Robert Mackenzie

Oliver & Boyd

Oliver & Boyd
Robert Stevenson House
1–3 Baxter's Place
Edinburgh EH1 3BB

A Division of Longman Group UK Ltd

© Oliver & Boyd 1989

ISBN 0 05 004185 1

First published 1989

Set in Linotron 202 10/11pt Plantin and 9/11pt Universe

Produced by Longman Group (F.E.) Ltd
and printed in Hong Kong

Acknowledgements

The author and publishers are grateful to those listed below for permission to reproduce the following:

Aerofilms, photograph: 9; Birmingham Museum and Art Gallery, photograph: 90; Bridgeman Art Library, photographs: cover, 54, 107; BBC Hulton Picture Library, photographs: 28, 29, 30, 35, 39, 44, 45, 48 (2), 50, 58 (top), 63, 64 (bottom), 74 (right), 80, 86, 92 (top), 93, 96, 135, 136; Trustees of the British Museum, photographs: 13, 15, 17, 20, 24, 47, 73; Syndics of Cambridge University Library, photograph: 137 (bottom); Durham County Library, photograph: 71 (bottom); Fotomas Index, photographs: 27, 77; Robert Fleming Holding Limited, photograph: 105 (top); Stephen Gibson, map and table: 18, 39; Glasgow Art Gallery and Museum; photograph: 105 (bottom); Greater London Record Office, photograph: 84; Illustrated London News Picture Library, photographs: 32, 49, 83, 100, 118 (2), 123, 125; British Transport Historical Records, photograph: 122; Lady Longford, photograph: 20; Manchester Public Library, photographs: 75 (2); Mander & Mitchenson Theatre Collection, photograph: 133 (top); Mansell Collection, photographs: 6–7, 10, 11, 23 (2), 36 (2), 42, 43, 46, 55, 58 (bottom), 60 (2), 62, 64 (top), 74 (left), 97, 98, 99, 116, 131 (bottom); Mary Evans Picture Library, photographs: 95, 119; Trustees of the National Library of Scotland, photographs: 61, 65, 120, 121; National Museums & Galleries on Merseyside, Walker Art Gallery, photograph, 34; National Trust Photographic Library, photograph: 128; *Punch*, photographs: 37 (2), 57, 85 (bottom), 87, 92 (bottom), 129, 131 (top), 137 (top), 138; Royal Holloway College, photograph: 107; Trustees of the Science Museum (London), photographs: 108, 109 (2), 110, 113 (2), 114; Sheffield City Libraries, photograph: 85 (top); W. H. Smith Ltd, photograph: 126; Trustees of the Victoria and Albert Museum, photographs: 132, 133 (bottom), 134; Weidenfeld & Nicolson Archives, photograph: 20; Wellcome Institute for the History of Medicine, photographs: 56, 71 (top).

Design and maps on pages 102, 112 by Cauldron Design Studio

Introduction

This is a textbook for students of the topic *Britain 1815–51* in a GCSE History course. The book deals with the changes and continuity within the period and the forces and individuals that helped shape it.

A wide range of contemporary sources are used throughout. These have been carefully chosen to help develop the skills that the GCSE History course requires. In the sections Using the Evidence and Coursework, students can analyse and evaluate the source materials to weigh contrasting views of events and issues, distinguish biased opinions from statements of fact, and reach their own considered judgements and conclusions. The Coursework in every chapter also helps with the requirements of the GCSE course.

Through this process of historical investigation, students can see the period from the perspective of people living then, and with the benefit of hindsight, from that of the present day.

While directly aimed at GCSE candidates, this book will also be useful for all those in secondary school who are studying Britain in the first half of the nineteenth century.

Contents

Chairing the Member (William Hogarth)

1 The Vote

The Old Parliamentary System

In Britain today all adults can vote. The only qualification for the franchise (right to vote) is that the person should be over 18 years of age.

The parliamentary system of the early nineteenth century was very different. In the first place, there were many different qualifications for the vote, varying from place to place. One result of such qualifications was that the number of people who could vote was very small – less than half a million in 1831, out of a population of 24 million. Secondly, there were two different types of constituency (the area an MP represents). These were the counties and the boroughs. In England each county and borough, no matter their size, had two MPs; in Scotland MPs were shared, although most counties did have one each.

The franchise

Source 1.1 ... the members for the 52 counties are all elected by one uniform right. Every man throughout England, possessed of 40 shillings per annum freehold [land] ... is entitled to a vote ...

With respect to the different cities, towns, and boroughs, they exercise a variety of separate and distinct rights ... an infinite diversity of peculiar customs is to be found. In some places the number of voters is limited to a select body not exceeding 30 or 40; in others it is extended to 8 or 10 000. The remaining rights of voting are of a still more complicated description. Burgageholds [occupancy of a certain house], leaseholds, and freeholds, scot and lot [church and poor rates], inhabitants house-holders, inhabitants at large, potwallopers [owners of a hearth big enough to boil a pot] ... each in different boroughs prevail, and create endless misunderstandings ...

(*Report of the Society of the Friends of the People*, 9 February 1793)

Source 1.2 Glasgow's number of inhabitants exceeds 77 000; its delegate is chosen by thirty-two members of the town council, who are all self-elected; and this delegate has only one voice of four in the choice of a member of Parliament with the delegates of three little towns [Dumbarton, Renfrew and Rutherglen].

Of fifteen members for the cities and burghs, one for Edinburgh is chosen by thirty-three persons; the other fourteen by sixty-five delegates, who are elected by 1220 persons.

The inhabitants of Scotland are above two million; their representatives are chosen by 3844.

(T.H.B. Oldfield, *The Representative History of Great Britain and Ireland*, vol. VI pp. 190–3)

Many boroughs had fewer voters than even Glasgow or Edinburgh; for example, Sir Philip Francis gave an account of his election at Appleby in 1802:

Source 1.3 The Fact is that yesterday morning between 11 & 12 I was unanimously elected by one Elector, to represent this Ancient Borough in Parliament . . . There was no other Candidate, no Opposition, no Poll demanded, Scrutiny, or petition. So I had nothing to do but thank the said Elector for the Unanimous Voice by which I was chosen. On Friday Morning I shall quit this Triumphant Scene with flying Colours and a noble Determination not to see it again in less than seven years.

(*Francis Letters*, vol. II, p. 493; in Julius West, *A History of the Chartist Movement*, p. 14)

The constituencies

Nowadays, an attempt is made to make constituencies as nearly equal in population as possible, so that people are represented by an MP on a fairly equal basis. This was not the case in the early nineteenth century.

Source 1.4 The Old Parliamentary System

The Old Parliamentary System

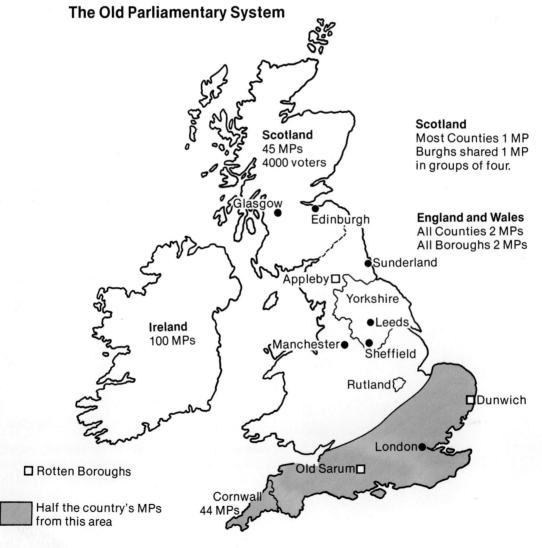

Scotland
45 MPs
4000 voters

Glasgow
Edinburgh

Scotland
Most Counties 1 MP
Burghs shared 1 MP
in groups of four.

England and Wales
All Counties 2 MPs
All Boroughs 2 MPs

Sunderland
Appleby □
Yorkshire
Leeds
Manchester ● Sheffield
Rutland

Ireland
100 MPs

□ Dunwich

Rutland

London ●

Old Sarum □

□ **Rotten Boroughs**

Half the country's MPs from this area

Cornwall
44 MPs

Source 1.5 A stranger ... would be very much astonished if he were taken to a ruined mound, and told that that mound sent two representatives to Parliament – if he were taken to a stone wall and told that three niches in it sent two representatives to Parliament – if he were taken to a park, where no houses were to be seen, and told that that park sent two representatives: but if he were told this and were astonished at hearing it, he would be still more astonished if he were to see large and opulent towns full of enterprise and industry, and intelligence, containing vast magazines of every species of manufactures, and were told that these towns sent no representatives to Parliament.

(Speech in the House of Lords by Lord John Russell, 1831)

Source 1.6 The county of Yorkshire, which contains nearly a million of souls, sends two country members; and so does Rutland, which contains not an hundredth part of that number. The town of Old Sarum, which contains not three houses, sends two members; and the town of Manchester, which contains upwards of sixty thousand souls, is not admitted to send any. Is there any principle in these things?

(Thomas Paine, *Rights of Man*, 1791)

Source 1.7 Old Sarum is an area about one hundred yards in diameter taking in the whole crown of a hill. Near this is one farm house, which is all that remains of any town in or near the place, for the encampment has no resemblance of a town; and yet this is called the borough of Old Sarum, and sends two members to Parliament; who these members can justly say they represent, would be hard for them to answer.

(Daniel Defoe, *A Tour through the Whole Island of Great Britain*, 1726)

Source 1.8 Old Sarum

Source 1.9 The Polling (Hogarth)

Elections

Only landowners could stand for Parliament. Many seats were pocket boroughs, controlled by one family, so a choice of candidates there was rare. Sometimes the two political parties, the Tories and the Whigs, would agree to share a constituency, sending one MP each. Where elections did actually take place, they were dominated by bribery and corruption.

Source 1.10 At Nottingham, one gentleman confessed to having paid away in the election of 1826, above £3000 in bribery in a single day. At Leicester, the voters, in anticipation of a contest, expressed their hope that the price of votes might rise to £10, as they said it commonly did, if the struggle was severe.

(*The Extraordinary Blue Book*, 1831)

Source 1.11 Some seats are private property; the right of voting belongs to a few householders . . . and . . . these votes are commanded by the owner of the estate. The fewer they are, the more easily they are managed . . . Where the number of voters is greater . . . the business is more difficult and . . . expensive. The candidate . . . must deal individually with the constituents, who sell themselves to the highest bidder . . .

(Robert Southey, *Letters from England*, 1807)

Source 1.12 971. Have you ever known intimidation practiced to any extent at a county election? – Yes, by landlords over tenants.
972. In what ways have they exercised that intimidation? – By insisting upon their voting as the landlord wished, and it was perfectly understood by them that they would lose their farms if they voted contrary to the wishes and inclinations of their landlords . . .

(Report of the Select Committee on Bribery at Elections, *Parliamentary Papers*, 1835, viii, pp. 58–9)

Source 1.13 Show of Hands for a Liberal Candidate (George Cruikshank)

Charles Dickens described an imaginary election in one of his novels:

Source 1.14 During the whole time of the polling, the town was in a perpetual fever of excitement. Exciseable articles were remarkably cheap at all the public houses; and spring vans paraded the streets for the accommodation of voters who were seized with any temporary dizziness in the head – an epidemic which prevailed among the electors, during the contest, to a most alarming extent, and under the influence of which they might frequently be seen lying on the pavements in a state of utter insensibility. A small body of electors remained unpolled on the very last day. They were calculating and reflecting persons, who had not yet been convinced by the arguments of either party, although they had had frequent conferences with each. One hour before the close of the poll, Mr Perker [Slumkey's agent] solicited the honour of a private interview with these intelligent, these noble, these patriotic men. It was granted. His arguments were brief, but satisfactory. They went in a body to the poll; and when they returned, the honourable Samuel Slumkey, of Slumkey Hall, was returned also.

(Charles Dickens, *The Posthumous Papers of the Pickwick Club*, 1901 edition, pp. 136–7)

The *Observer* newspaper reported on an actual election:

Source 1.15 The election for the Borough of Finsbury commenced, on Islington-green, where spacious hustings were erected . . .

The CLERK to the RETURNING OFFICER came forward to take the opinions of the electors with regard to the fitness of the several candidates. He first desired all those who were not electors to take their departure from the ground on pain of imprisonment, but, as may be supposed, no one paid attention to the command. He then called on the electors to hold up their hands on his calling out the name of each candidate . . . A tolerable number of hands appeared for Mr Babbage, a greater number for Mr Temple, about the same number for Mr Grant, a very few for Mr Serjeant Spankie and a great number for Mr Wakely. It is but fair to state, that many boys and others, who certainly could not be electors, held up their hands. The Returning Officer declared that the election had fallen on Thomas Wakely Esq. and the Right Honourable R. Grant. Some uproar followed this, many contending that Mr Temple had a larger show of hands than Mr Grant . . .

The three remaining candidates then demanded a poll, which the Returning Officer acceded [agreed] to . . .

(The *Observer*, 10 December 1832)

The following week, the *Observer* reported the result of the poll:

Source 1.16   THE MEMBERS DECLARED

On Wednesday Mr Satchell announced the numbers as follows:

Mr Grant	4278	Mr Wakely	2151
Mr Serjeant Spankie	2848	Mr Temple	787
Mr Babbage	2311		

Mr Satchell stated, amidst cheers and some groaning from the crowd, that the election had fallen on the Right Honourable Robert Grant and Mr Serjeant Spankie.

(The *Observer*, 16 December 1832)

Another writer commented on the Finsbury election:

Source 1.17   . . . look at our Metropolitan Elections; compare the results as demonstrated by show of hands, with the results as shown by the polls; see everywhere a forest of hands for the honest candidate and see him afterwards demolished when left to the skulking votes . . . In Finsbury the show of hands for Mr Wakely was immense . . . We all know the result of the poll . . . Had there been universal or even householders' suffrage [right to vote] Mr Wakely would have been sent by an overwhelming majority . . .

(*Poor Man's Guardian* 15 December 1832)

_____ **Using the Evidence** _____

1. From sources 1.1, 1.2 and 1.3 write a brief report summarising all the problems with the franchise.

2. From sources 1.4 to 1.8 answer the following
   (a) How many MPs did each county and borough in England have?
   (b) The map shows that Cornwall had 44 MPs. How many boroughs were there in Cornwall? Explain your answer.
   (c) Why, according to Lord John Russell, would a stranger be astonished if he were shown parts of England?
   (d) According to Thomas Paine, Old Sarum had two MPs while Manchester had none. How do you think such a situation came about? Remember that the parliamentary system had remained unchanged for centuries.
   (e) Old Sarum was one of many 'rotten boroughs'. Use the picture and extracts to describe Old Sarum, and explain why 'rotten Borough' was a suitable description for places like Old Sarum.

3. Look at source 1.9. What do you think the artist is trying to show in this picture?

4. Look at sources 1.10, 1.11 and 1.12.
   (a) From source 1.10 why did the voters of Leicester hope for a close election?
   (b) From source 1.11 how did a voter decide which candidate to vote for?
   (c) From source 1.12 how could landlords control who their tenants voted for?

5. Look at source 1.13.
   (a) What are the '50 000 reasons' which the candidate is offering?
   (b) What purpose do you think the barrels of gin and beer would serve?
   (c) Do the voters appear interested in politics? Explain your answer.
   (d) What message is the cartoonist trying to put forward about
       (i) the sort of people that would get elected
       (ii) the reasons why people voted for a particular candidate?

6. Look at source 1.14. What do you think Charles Dickens was trying to achieve, by describing an election in this way?

7. Look at sources 1.15, 1.16, 1.17.
   (a) From sources 1.15 and 1.16 compare the result produced by the show of hands with the result in the poll.
   (b) What reasons can you suggest for the differing results?
   (c) How would the changes proposed by the writer in source 1.17 make bribery more difficult?

The Corn Laws

Parliament thus was dominated by the landowners who made up both political parties, the Tories and the Whigs. Few middle- or working-class people could even vote. The result was that Parliament usually only concerned itself with the interests of the landowners. The passing of the Corn Laws in 1815 provides an example.

During the long wars with France, which lasted from the early 1790s to 1815, Britain was unable to import wheat from the Continent. The country thus had to depend on home-grown wheat to produce the bread most people lived on. The effects can be seen in the table:

Source 1.18   Prices of Wheat and Bread, 1785–1814

Year	Wheat Prices (shillings per quarter)	Bread Prices (Pence per loaf)
1785–89	44.92	6.1
1790–94	49.57	6.6
1795–99	65.67	8.8
1800–04	84.85	11.7
1805–09	84.57	12.2
1810–14	102.47	14.6

The landowners in Parliament also expected the end of the war to affect the price of the wheat they – or their tenant farmers – sold; so in 1815 Parliament passed the Corn Laws. These stated that no foreign wheat could be sold in Britain until the price of home-grown wheat reached 80 shillings a quarter.

Source 1.19   Everybody must have observed that families with four or five young children are common in country parishes. As bread makes the principal part of the food of all poor families, and almost the whole of the food in all such large families, it is manifest [obvious] that whatever causes operate in raising at any time the price of corn, the same must necessarily bring heavy distress upon families of this description.

(Rev. D. Davies, quoted in E. G. Power, *Robert Peel Free Trade and the Corn Laws*, p. 42)

Source 1.20   . . . a series of disturbances commenced with the introduction of the Corn Bill, and continued with short intervals, until the close of the year 1816. In London and Westminster riots ensued [followed] and were continued for several days, whilst the bill was discussed. At Bridgeport there were riots on account of the high price of bread . . . and December 7th 1816, at Dundee, where, owing to the high price of meal, upwards of one hundred shops were plundered.

(Samuel Bamford, *Passages in the Life of a Radical*, 2nd edition, 1840, p. 6)

Source 1.21   The Blessings of Peace (Cruikshank)

1. Look at source 1.18. Describe what has happened to the prices of bread and wheat from 1785 to 1814.

2. Look at source 1.19. Who suffered most from the prices of wheat imposed by the Corn Laws?

3. From source 1.20 what does Samuel Bamford give as the reasons for the events he described?

4. From source 1.21
   (a) The man near the right is 'John Bull' who often represents the 'typical Englishman' in cartoons. What sort of state is his family in?
   (b) According to 'John Bull' what is the only solution for such families?
   (c) How does the cartoonist show that corn was plentiful on the Continent?
   (d) Using words and his drawing, the cartoonist makes his feelings about the landowners clear. Describe the cartoonist's feelings using all the evidence you can find.

The Radicals

The passing of the Corn Laws was just one of many reasons for discontent in the years after 1815. Poor people also complained about unemployment, high taxes and dreadful working and living conditions. The Tory government that was in power from 1812 to 1830 was not interested in the problems of the poor; as we have seen, they passed laws like the Corn Laws to protect their own interests.

Some people felt that the only way that Parliament would pass laws to help the poor would be if the poor were actually represented in Parliament. People who believed in such sweeping reforms were known as Radicals. One of the best-known Radicals was William Cobbett who published a newspaper called the *Weekly Political Register* – his opponents referred to it as the 'Twopenny Trash'. In the *Political Register*, Cobbett attacked the government and spelled out what was needed to help the people:

Source 1.22 At this time the writings of William Cobbett suddenly became of great authority; they were read on nearly every cottage hearth in the manufacturing districts of South Lancashire; in those of Leicester, Derby and Nottingham; also in many of the Scottish manufacturing towns. Their influence was speedily visible; he directed his readers to the true cause of their sufferings – misgovernment; and to its proper corrective – parliamentary reform.

(Bamford, p. 11)

Source 1.23 The remedy [cure] is what we now have to look to, and that remedy consists wholly and solely of such a reform in the Commons' or People's House of Parliament, as shall give to every payer of direct taxes a vote at elections, and as shall cause the Members to be elected annually . . .

(*Weekly Political Register*, 2 November 1816)

Throughout the period from 1815 to 1820 people held meetings and organized marches to protest about their grievances. Henry Hunt became the best-known Radical speaker and was nicknamed 'the Orator'. The government was very worried about such protests. Its members feared that bloody revolution might break out in Britain as had happened in France in 1789. They took a number of measures to prevent this happening. In 1817 *Habeas Corpus* was suspended; this meant that anyone could be arrested and jailed just on suspicion, and without a trial. Faced with arrest, William Cobbett fled to America. The Home Secretary, Lord Sidmouth, did not have a police force to keep law and order, so he relied on spies to tell him what was happening. Sometimes these spies actually encouraged Radical plots and then reported them to the authorities. The government also used troops to break up meetings and marches.

Source 1.24 Death or Liberty!

Using the Evidence

1. Look at source 1.22. What sort of people read the *Political Register*?

2. Look at source 1.23. Why do you think Radicals wanted such frequent elections?

3. Source 1.24 shows the 'fair Britannia' under attack by 'Radical Reform'.
   (a) What sort of values does Britannia stand for?
   (b) What figure is used to represent 'Radical Reform'?
   (c) What do the figures following 'Radical Reform' represent?
   (d) How is 'Radical Reform's' true appearance concealed?
   (e) The cartoonist is suggesting that the Radicals also concealed their true appearance. What did he think the Radicals really wanted?
   (f) Which people would have agreed with the views in the cartoon?

'Peterloo', 1819

Workers from all over the Manchester area gathered in St Peter's Fields Manchester on 16 August 1819 to hear Radical speakers such as Henry 'Orator' Hunt. In all, about 80 000 people gathered from Manchester and the surrounding towns.

Source 1.25 The place appointed for the meeting was a large vacant piece of ground on the north side of St Peter's Place . . . About half-past eleven the first body of Reformers arrived on the ground, bearing two banners . . . The first bore upon a white ground the inscription 'Annual Parliaments, and Universal Suffrage'; on the reverse side: 'No Corn Laws'. The other bore upon a blue ground the same inscription, with the addition of 'Vote by Ballot' . . . Numerous large bodies of Reformers continued to arrive from this time to one o'clock, from the different towns in the neighbourhood of Manchester, all with white flags, and many of them drawn up five deep, and in regular marching order . . .

(The Times, 19 August 1819)

Samuel Bamford explained that an extra effort had been made to ensure that the gathering would be orderly and peaceful:

Source 1.26 . . . Order in our movement was obtained by drilling; and peace . . . was secured by a prohibition [ban] of all weapons . . . Thus our arrangements were soon rendered perfect and ten thousand men moved with the regularity of ten score . . .

Our whole column, with the Rochdale·people, would probably consist of six thousand men. A hundred or two of our handsomest girls . . . danced to the music, or sung snatches of popular songs; a score or two of children were sent back, though some went forward; whilst on each side of our line walked some thousands of stragglers. And thus . . . we went slowly towards Manchester.

(Bamford; p. 165)

The local magistrates were worried about the planned meeting in case it led to rioting, so they too had made preparations. A small force of special constables was raised, and it would be backed up by a troop of regular Hussars, and by the Manchester and Salford Yeomanry, a local volunteer force made up from middle-class businessmen and tradesmen. The magistrates allowed Hunt to start his speech, then decided to arrest him. As Hunt was being arrested,

Source 1.27 . . . a noise and strange murmur arose . . . Some persons said it was the Blackburn people coming, and I stood on tip-toe . ., and saw a party of cavalry in blue and white uniform, come trotting sword in hand . . . to the front of a row of new houses, where they reined up in a line . . .

On the cavalry drawing up they were received with a shout of goodwill, as I understood it. They shouted again, waving their sabres over their heads; and then, slackening rein, and striking spur into their steeds, they dashed forward, and began cutting the people.

. . . and their sabres were plied to hew a way through naked held-up hands, and defenceless heads; and then chopped limbs, and wound-gaping skulls were seen; and groans and cries were mingled with the din of that horrid confusion . . .

On the breaking of the crowd, the yeomanry wheeled; and dashing wherever there was an opening, they followed, pressing and wounding . . . Women, white-vested maids, and tender youths, were indiscriminately sabred or trampled . . .

In ten minutes from the commencement of the havoc, the field was an open and almost deserted place . . . The hustings remained, with a few broken and hewed flag-staves erect, and a torn and gashed banner or two dropping; whilst over the whole field, were strewed caps, bonnets, hats, shawls and shoes, and other parts of male and female dress; trampled, torn and bloody . . . Several mounds of human beings still remained where they had fallen, crushed down, and smothered. Some of these still groaning – others with staring eyes, were gasping for breath, and others would never breathe more. All was silent save those low sounds . . .

(Bamford, pp. 166–8)

Eleven people were killed, and about 400 seriously injured. Hunt was sentenced to two years imprisonment, and the magistrates congratulated by Lord Sidmouth, the Home Secretary. Throughout Britain, there was a tremendous outcry against the government, and the 'victory' was scornfully referred to as the 'Battle of Peterloo'.

The government refused to set up an enquiry into 'Peterloo'. Instead they used it as an excuse to pass even harsher measures against the Radicals. These became known as the Six Acts. Under these Acts:
– military training and drilling was banned
– magistrates were given powers to search for arms
– trials were to be brought about more quickly
– people could only attend meetings within their own parishes

- newspapers came under strict government controls
- all newspapers and pamphlets were to be subject to Stamp duty, thus making them more expensive.

Who was to blame?

How could such a tragedy have happened? Most witnesses believed they knew where the blame lay:

Source 1.28 A comparatively undisciplined body, led on by officers who had never had any experience in military affairs, and probably all under the influence both of personal fear and considerable political feeling of hostility, could not be expected to act either with coolness or discrimination; and accordingly men, women and children, constables and Reformers, were all equally exposed to their attacks.

(*The Times*. 19 August 1819)

Source 1.29 Was that [meeting] at Manchester an 'unlawful assembly'? Was the notice of it unlawful?

We believe not. Was the subject proposed for discussion [Parliamentary reform] an unlawful object? Assuredly not. Was any thing done at this meeting before the cavalry rode in upon it, either contrary to [against] law or in breach of the peace? No such circumstance is recorded in any of the statements which have reached our hands.

(*The Times*, 19 August 1819)

Source 1.30 When I got to the end of Watson street, I saw ten or twelve of the Yeomanry Cavalry, and two of the Hussars cutting at the people, who were wedged close together, when an officer of Hussars rode up to his own men, and knocking up their swords said, 'Damn you what do you mean by this work?' He then called out to the Yeomanry, 'For shame, gentlemen; what are you about? the people cannot get away.' They desisted [stopped] for a time, but no sooner had the officer rode to another part of the field, than they fell to work again.

(Quoted in E. P. Thompson, *The Making of the English Working Class*, p. 753)

Source 1.31 Britons Strike Home (Cruikshank)

1. (a) From source 1.25 write down four of the demands of the people attending the meeting.

2. From source 1.26.
   (a) What preparations had been made to make sure that the crowds of protesters went to the meeting in an orderly way?
   (b) Why do you think they thought it was important to have orderly marches?
   (c) Can you suggest how these preparations might give the authorities a wrong impression?
   (d) Note down all the points which suggest that the Radicals did intend the meeting to be peaceful.

3. Look at source 1.27. Find three different ways in which people were injured or killed. Use this information to explain why there were so many casualties.

4. Look at source 1.28. The Yeomanry is being described here. How were they different from the Hussars? What effect might this have, if they were in a difficult situation?

5. From source 1.29 does the extract from *The Times* support or oppose the possibility that it was the cavalry, not the people, that started the violence?

6. Sources 1.30 and 1.31 suggest that the Yeomanry may have had deeper reasons for their action:
   (a) From source 1.30
       (i) What did the officer of Hussars think of the Yeomanry's action? What did they do once he had gone?
       (ii) Were the Yeomanry in danger themselves? Why, then, do you think they 'fell to work again'?
   (b) From source 1.31
       (i) What do you notice about the appearance of the Yeomanry?
       (ii) What two reasons does the officer use to encourage his men to 'Chop 'em down!'?
       (iii) Who do you think would produce a cartoon like this, and what purpose do you think it was meant to serve?
       (iv) Does the cartoon serve any use as a source for a historian studying 'Peterloo'? Explain your answer.

_____ **Coursework** _____

Empathy

For this exercise you will need to form a group of four. Each member of the group tries to explain what happened and why it happened from the point of view of one of the people concerned:
  (i) a Manchester magistrate
  (ii) the Home Secretary, Lord Sidmouth
  (iii) a member of the Manchester Yeomanry
  (iv) one of the 'Reformers'.

Catholic Emancipation

The Tory party continued to resist all demands for a reform of the parliamentary system. They still believed that landowners were the best people to run the country. However, before the end of their long period as the government they were pushed into changing one aspect of the system. This concerned the position of Roman Catholics.

According to laws dating back to the seventeenth century, Catholics were unable to become Members of Parliament. This barrier was especially resented in Ireland where three-quarters of the population were Catholic.

In 1801 by the Act of Union, Ireland lost its own Parliament, and joined with Great Britain to form the 'United Kingdom'. Ireland's MPs now sat in the Westminster Parliament.

In 1823 a Dublin lawyer, Daniel O'Connell, founded the Catholic Association. Its aim was to force the government to grant Catholic emancipation, giving Catholics the freedom to sit in Parliament. In 1828 O'Connell himself stood for election in County Clare against a popular Tory landowner, W. Vesey Fitzgerald:

Source 1.32 Fellow Countrymen,
Your country wants a representative . . .
Of my qualification to fill that station, I leave you to judge. The habits of public speaking and many, many years of public business, render me, perhaps equally suited with most men to attend to the interests of Ireland in Parliament.

You will be told I am not qualified to be elected: the assertion, my friends, is untrue. I am qualified to be elected, and to be your representative. It is true that as a Catholic, I cannot, and of course never will, take the oaths at present prescribed to members of Parliament; but . . . I entertain a confident hope that if you elect me, the most bigotted of our enemies will see the necessity of removing from the chosen representative of the people, an obstacle from doing his duty to his King and to his country.

(Daniel O'Connell's Election Address, in R. Huish,
Memoirs of Daniel O'Connell, p. 438)

O'Connell won the election easily, but, as the law stood, he could not take his seat in Parliament. Most Tories were confident that the Prime Minister, the Duke of Wellington, and his Home Secretary, Sir Robert Peel, were men who could be relied on to resist the Catholic demands; but both were aware of the danger of sticking to this policy:

Source 1.33 I have opposed what is called Catholic Emancipation . . . But whatever may be my opinion upon these points, I cannot deny that the state of Ireland under existing circumstances is most unsatisfactory.

(Sir Robert Peel in August 1828; in C. S. Parker,
Sir Robert Peel, vol. II, p. 55)·

Faced then, with the threat of open rebellion in Ireland if O'Connell did not take his seat, Wellington and Peel persuaded their colleagues (and the reluctant King George IV) to pass the Catholic Relief Act:

Source 1.34 . . . from and after the commencement of this Act it shall be lawful for any person professing the Roman Catholic Religion to sit and vote in either House of Parliament, being in all other respects duly qualified . . .

(Public General Statutes, 1829; in Norman Gash, *The Age of Peel*, p. 29)

Source 1.35 Oh! Member for Oxford! you shuffle and wheel! You have altered your name from R. Peel to Repeal.

(*Birmingham Argus*, January 1829, quoted in,
Asa Briggs, *The Age of Improvement*, 1959)

Using the Evidence

1. Look at source 1.32. If O'Connell won, he would be unable to take his seat in Parliament; so what was his reason for standing?

2. Using sources 1.32 to 1.35 answer the following:
   (a) Why was it surprising that this particular government granted Catholic Emancipation?
   (b) How do you explain their change of mind?

3. Look at source 1.35. What do you think some Tories thought of this change of mind by their leaders? What effect would this have on the Tory Party?

Source 1.36 Land Lubbers & Over Laden (Heath)

Source 1.37 The System that Works so Well (Cruickshank)

Attitudes to reform

Although the Tories had been forced into granting Catholic Emancipation, they had no intention of passing any further reforms of the parliamentary system. The existing system suited them well enough. Many Tories believed that only landowners were fit people to take part in government.

Source 1.38 I am satisfied with the constitution [system of government] under which I have lived hitherto, which I believe is adapted to the wants and habits of the people ... I will continue my opposition [to reform] ... believing, as I do, that this is the first step, not directly to revolution, but to a series of changes which will affect the property, and totally change the character, of the mixed constitution of this country ...

(Robert Peel, Speech in House of Commons, 17 December 1831)

Source 1.39 I, on my own part, will go further, and say, that I never read or heard of any measure ... which in any degree satisfies my mind that the state of representation can be improved ... I will go further and say, that the Legislature [Parliament] and the system of representation possesses the full and entire confidence of the country ... Under these circumstances ... I am not only not prepared to bring forward any measure [of reform] but I will at once declare that ... I shall always feel it my duty to resist such measures when proposed by others.

(Duke of Wellington, Speech in House of Lords, 2 November 1830)

Radical demands were best summed up by William Cobbett:

Source 1.40 It will be asked, will a reform of Parliament give the labouring man a cow or a pig; will it put bread or cheese into his satchel instead of infernal cold potatoes; will it give him a bottle of beer to carry to the field instead of making him lie down on his belly to drink out of the brook ...? Will Parliamentary Reform put an end to the harnessing of men and women by a hired overseer to draw carts like beasts of burden; will it put an end to the system which causes the honest labourer to be worst fed than the felons in the jails? ... The enemies of reform jeeringly ask us, whether reform would do these things for us; and I answer distinctly THAT IT WOULD DO THEM ALL.

(William Cobbett, *Political Register*, 1832)

The middle class were also pressing for parliamentary reform. In 1830, a Birmingham banker, Thomas Atwood, formed the Birmingham Political Union:

Source 1.41 That honourable House [of Commons], in its present state, is evidently too far removed in habits, wealth and station, from the wants and interests of the lower and middle classes of the people, to have ... any close identity of feeling with them. The great aristocratical interests of all kinds are well represented there. The landed interest, the church, the law, the monied interest ... the members of that honourable House being all immediately and closely connected with these great interests. But the interests of Industry and of Trade have scarcely any representatives at all! These, the most vital interests of the nation, the source of all its wealth and of all its strength, are comparatively unrepresented ...

(Declaration of the Birmingham Political Union, 1830, p. 7)

Some Whigs also favoured parliamentary reform. Although they were also landowners they were worried about the danger of a revolution in Britain. Two things made this fear very real in 1830. In the south of England, bad harvests and extreme poverty had led to outbreaks of violence and machine-breaking among agricultural labourers. In the summer of 1830 the French King had been overthrown in a revolution led by the middle class:

Source 1.42 I support this measure [of reform] because I am sure that it is our best security against a revolution ... At present we oppose the schemes of revolutionists with only one half, with only one quarter of our proper force. We say, and we say justly, that it is not by mere numbers, but by property and intelligence that the nation ought to be governed. Yet, saying this, we exclude from all share in the government vast masses of property and intelligence, vast numbers of those who are most interested in preserving tranquillity [peace] and who know best how to preserve it. We do more. We drive over to the side of revolution those whom we shut out from power. Is this a time when the cause of law and order can spare one of its natural allies?

Turn where we may ... the voice of great events is proclaiming to us, 'Reform, that you may preserve' ...

(T. B. Macaulay, Speech in the House of Commons, 2 March 1831)

1. Source 1.36 shows the Prime Minister, the Duke of Wellington, at sea with his 'crew', their boat weighed down with millstones.
   (a) What name would we give to Wellington's 'crew' in Parliament?
   (b) Which millstone has been thrown overboard? Briefly explain how that had come about.
   (c) Do any of the 'crew' want further reform? Explain your answer.
   (d) By suggesting that they are 'Land Lubbers' at sea, what point is the cartoonist making about Wellington and his crew?

2. St Stephen's, the mill in source 1.37, represents Parliament.
   (a) (i) Who is providing the power that turns the wheel?
       (ii) What sort of names are on the wheel?
   (b) (i) What does the 'mill' produce?
       (ii) Who benefits from it?
   (c) How is the 'mill' supported? Explain the point the cartoonist is making by these 'supports'. You should be able to illustrate your answer by referring to an actual event.
   (d) What reason do the supporters of the system in the cartoon give for wanting to keep things unchanged?
   (e) Do you think the cartoonist believed the 'System worked Well'? Give a full explanation for your answer.

3. Look at source 1.38. Briefly explain in your own words Peel's reason for opposing changes in the parliamentary system.

4. Look at sources 1.36 and 1.39. Did Wellington's 'crew' entirely share his view of the system?

5. Look at source 1.40. How could parliamentary reform do any of the things that Cobbett claimed?

6. Look at source 1.41. In what way does Atwood's statement disagree with Peel and Wellington (sources 1.38 & 1.39)?

7. Look at source 1.42. Explain exactly what was meant by the last five words of this extract.

The Time-table of Reform

Although the Tories won the general election of 1830 narrowly, they were defeated soon after. The Whigs formed a government with Earl Grey as Prime Minister. The Whigs had promised parliamentary reform during the election campaign, and now prepared a bill.

Nov. 1830 – Tory government fell from power; Whigs formed government.

Mar. 1831 – Lord John Russell presented a reform bill to the House of Commons, but the bill was defeated, so the government resigned.

May 1831 – General Election – Whigs returned with increased majority.

Oct. 1831 – Second attempt at Reform defeated by House of Lords. The country erupted in fury, with riots in Bristol, Derby and Nottingham.

May 1832 – Third Reform Bill interfered with by Lords. Grey now asked the King to create 50 new Whig peers (members of the House of Lords) in order to swamp the Tory majority there. The King would only permit 20, so government resigned.

The 'May Days' – The King now asked the Duke of Wellington to form a government. This led to renewed riots and protests throughout the country.

The Birmingham Political Union announced that 200 000 men would march on London and stay there until reform was passed. People put up signs saying: 'No taxes paid here till the Reform Bill is passed'. Francis Place urged people: 'To Stop the Duke Go for Gold' – he hoped that if enough people withdrew their money from the banks there would be a financial crisis. Faced with this widespread opposition, Wellington informed the King that he was unable to form a government.

May 1832 – Grey returned as Prime Minister, armed with a promise from the King to create new Whig peers if necessary, but Wellington now urged his party not to oppose the bill.

June 1832 – The Reform Act became law.

Source 1.44 The burning of Nottingham Castle, October 1831

Source 1.43 The Bristol Reform Riots, October 1831

Source 1.45 Up and Down or Political See-saw

_____ **Using the Evidence** _____

1. Study 'The Time-table of Reform' (p. 22) and sources 1.43, 1.44 and 1.45:
   (a) How could the political situation in 1832 be likened to a see-saw?
   (b) What is 'John Bull' doing in the cartoon? Why has the cartoonist put him in that position?
   (c) What is meant by Wellington's warning to the King?
   (d) Do you think the situation _was_ dangerous? Use all the available evidence in your answer.
   (e) What does the King's reply suggest about his attitude to parliamentary reform?
   (f) Do you think source 1.45 gives an accurate picture of the events of May 1832?

The Reform Act

The Act brought about two main changes, affecting the franchise and the distribution of parliamentary seats.

The 'new' franchise

In the _counties_, two new groups of voters joined the 40s. freeholders – the £10 copyholders (an old form of lease); and the £50 leaseholders.

The greatest change affected the *borough* franchise, where, as we have seen, a great number of qualifications existed:

Source 1.46 . . . in every City or Borough which shall return a Member or Members to serve in any future Parliament, every Male Person of full Age, and not subject to any legal Incapacity, who shall occupy . . . as Owner or Tenant, any House, Warehouse, Counting-House, Shop, or other Building, . . . of the clear yearly Value of not less than Ten Pounds shall . . . be entitled to vote in the Election of a Member or Members to serve in any future Parliament for such City or Borough . . .

(The Reform Act, 7 June 1832; in Gash, *Age of Peel*, p. 48)

Thus a single uniform qualification had been created in the boroughs, entitling the £10 householders to vote.

The distribution of seats

56 of the most 'rotten boroughs' (including Old Sarum, Appleby and Dunwich) lost both their MPs; 30 slightly less rotten boroughs lost one MP. With other small changes, this provided 145 seats to be redistributed.

These were given to the counties and cities of the north, so that for the first time towns such as Manchester, Sunderland, Leeds and Sheffield would have their own representatives in Parliament. Eight seats were given to the Scottish burghs, bringing Scotland's representation up to 53; five more seats were given to Ireland.

Effects of reform

The main effect of the Reform Act was to give the vote to the growing middle class. Many people welcomed the Act at first:

Source 1.47 Every sensible man sees that the Reform Bill is the commencement of a mighty revolution.

(Cobbett, *Political Register*, 7 July 1832)

Source 1.48 When the Bill is safe, we cannot think so ill of human nature as to think that those who will have gained their freedom, will not aid us to gain ours.

(*Poor Man's Guardian*, 26 May 1832)

Reactions to the Act soon began to change. People started to realise that it was not 'a mighty revolution'. The increase in the size of the electorate was small – from about 480 000 to 814 000 – so only one man in six had the vote. The south of England was still over-represented, while some 'pocket' and 'rotten' boroughs still existed. The Duke of Wellington felt encouraged:

Source 1.49 I don't think that the influence of property in this country is diminished. That is to say that the gentry have as many followers, and influence as many voters at elections as they ever did.

(Duke of Wellington: in L. J. Jennings (ed.), *The Croker Papers*)

The system of voting had not been changed:

Source 1.50 Intimidation is practiced in towns by the threat of taking away your own custom, and by inducing others, over whom you have influence, to take away theirs, too, and by a general threat of doing all the injury to the tradesmen within the range of your power.

('Report of the Select Committee on Bribery at Elections', *Parliamentary Papers*, 1835, viii, p. 59)

Source 1.51 Principle [honesty] is unknown among the electors, the far greater proportion of whom are free burgesses of the lowest order, and require feasting and treating and other weighty considerations to bring them to the poll.

(*Morning Chronicle*, 2 January 1835)

Source 1.52 We have often told you the Reform Bill would do you no good . . . The great majority of the new electors are middlemen who thrive by your degradation . . . Your thoroughgoing middleman is never a reformer . . .

(*Poor Man's Guardian*, 15 December 1832)

Source 1.53 Fellow Countrymen,
It is now nearly six years since the Reform Bill became a part of the laws of this country. To carry that measure . . . the co-operation of the millions was sought for and cheerfully given . . . Alas, their hopes were excited by promises which have not been kept, and their expectations of freedom have been bitterly disappointed . . .

(William Lovett, *Life and Struggles*, 1876, pp. 118–119)

1. (a) Look back at source 1.40 on p. 21. Did the Reform Act do what Cobbett hoped for there?
   (b) If not, explain why Cobbett and the *Poor Man's Guardian* both appear to favour it in sources 1.47 and 1.48 above.

2. Explain how the following people would feel about the Act by studying the source named:
   (a) Wellington and Peel – sources 1.38 and 1.39, p. 21.
   (b) Thomas Atwood – source 1.41, p. 21.
   (c) Macaulay and other Whigs – source 1.42, p. 21.

3. Look at sources 1.50 and 1.51. How did the sort of points referred to here make the Reform Act more acceptable to someone like the Duke of Wellington?

4. Look at source 1.52.
   (a) In what way does the writer here contradict the (different) writer of source 1.48 from the same newspaper?
   (b) Notice the date of source 1.52. Why do you think this writer now feels so strongly about the Act?

5. Look at source 1.53. From your knowledge so far, which of the statements in the final sentence of this source is more accurate? *Were* the workers 'excited by promises which were not kept' or was it their 'expectations' which were 'bitterly disappointed'?

Chartism

The 1832 Reform Act thus proved a great disappointment to the working class, since they had not got the vote. They hoped at least that it would be followed by laws to improve their living and working conditions but they were disappointed again. The 1833 Factory Act did nothing to help adults or improve conditions (see Chapter 3) while the Poor Law Amendment Act of 1834 was hated by the working class (see Chapter 2).

Some people believed that the only way to improve matters was to get working people elected to Parliament. Groups such as the London Working Men's Association and the factory workers of northern England and Scotland supported this idea. In 1836 William Lovett of the London Working Men's Association summed up their demands in a document which became known as the People's Charter. The Charter contained six points. Lovett and his supporters wanted Parliament to pass the six points of the Charter as new laws. The movement which developed to persuade Parliament to do so became known as Chartism, and its supporters, Chartists.

Working-class views of the Reform Act

Source 1.54 It was the fond expectation of the people that a remedy for the greater part, if not for the whole, of their grievances, would be found in the Reform Act of 1832.

They have been bitterly and basely deceived.

The fruit which looked so fair to the eye has turned to dust and ashes when gathered.

The Reform Act has effected [brought about] a transfer of power from one domineering faction [ruling group] to another, and left the people helpless as before.

(The Chartist Petition, 1838; in R. G. Gammage, *History of the Chartist Movement*, 1854, pp. 87–90)

Source 1.55 We were taught to look upon the Reform Act as the evergreen, from which would spring wholesome and imperishable fruit; the fact being that all which was before experimental in the way of tyranny has now become multiplied a thousand fold, and confirmed by permanent . . . law.

(*Northern Star*, 9 March 1839)

The Poor Law Amendment Act

Source 1.56 But the paramount [main] reason for

publishing the Book of the Bastiles was, the urgent necessity in the present alarming crisis – a crisis mainly attributable to [owing to] the operation of such harsh, biting statutes [laws] as the New Poor-Law – of calling the attention of the upper and middle classes to the inhumanity, unchristianity, injustice, and political and social danger of the continued administration of the New Poor-Law Amendment-Act in England and Wales.

Had there been no New Poor-Law, the name of Chartist would never have been heard . . .

(G. R. Wythen Baxter, *The Book of the Bastiles*, 1841, Introduction, p. iv)

Thomas Carlyle's view

Source 1.57 Chartism means the bitter discontent grown fierce and mad, the wrong condition therefore . . . of the Working Classes of England. It is a new name for a thing which has had many names, which will yet have many.

(Thomas Carlyle, *Chartism*, 1839 (1842 ed.) p. 2)

The Chartists' demands

Source 1.58 When the state calls for defenders, when it calls for money, no consideration of poverty or ignorance can be pleaded, in refusal of the call. . . . We perform the duties of freemen; we must have the privileges of freemen. Therefore we demand universal suffrage. The suffrage, to be exempt from [free from] the corruption of the wealthy and the violence of the powerful, must be secret.

(The Chartist Petition, 1838, in Gammage, p. 90)

Source 1.59 This question of Universal Suffrage was a knife and fork question after all; this question was a bread and cheese question . . . and if any man ask him what he meant by Universal Suffrage he would answer, that every working man in the land had a right to have a good coat on his back, a comfortable abode in which to shelter himself and his family, a good dinner upon his table, and no more work than was necessary for keeping him in health, and as much wages for that work as would keep him in plenty . . .

(Rev. J. R. Stephens at a Chartist meeting, reported in the *Northern Star*, 29 September 1838)

Source 1.60 The Six Points of the People's Charter

The Six Points
OF THE
PEOPLE'S
CHARTER.

. A vote for every man twenty-one years of age, of sound d, and not undergoing punishment for crime.

. The Ballot.—To protect the elector in the exercise of vote.

. No Property Qualification for Members of Parliament us enabling the constituencies to return the man of their ce, be he rich or poor.

. Payment of Members, thus enabling an honest trades-, working man, or other person, to serve a constituency, n taken from his business to attend to the interests of the try.

. Equal Constituencies, securing the same amount of esentation for the same number of electors, instead of ving small constituencies to swamp the votes of large ones.

. Annual Parliaments, thus presenting the most effectual k to bribery and intimidation, since though a constituency t be bought once in seven years (even with the ballot), no c could buy a constituency (under a system of universal age) in each ensuing twelvemonth; and since members, n elected for a year only, would not be able to defy and y their constituents as now.

Feargus O'Connor

Chartist methods

Throughout 1838 the Chartists held meetings to gain support for their petition, which they were to present to Parliament along with the Charter. Their best-known speaker was Feargus O'Connor, a fiery Irishman and owner of the northern England Radical newspaper, the *Northern Star*.

A Chartist Convention was held, with representatives from all the industrial areas of Britain. The petition was not yet complete, but it was well known that Parliament would reject it; so the Convention spent the first half of 1839 debating what should be done next. There were three main options:

Physical force

Source 1.61 *Feargus O'Connor's view*
Shall it be said, fellow countrymen, that four millions of men, capable of bearing arms, and defending their country against every foreign assailant, allowed a few domestic oppressors to enslave and degrade them? . . . We have resolved to gain our rights 'peacably if we may, forcibly if we must'; but woe to those who begin the warfare with the millions, or who forcibly resist their peaceful agitation for justice . . .

(*Northern Star*, 3 July 1847)

Source 1.62 *Julian Harney's advice*
To you that are not prepared I say again, ARM to protect your aged parents, ARM for your wives and children, ARM for your sweethearts and sisters, ARM to drive tyranny from the soil . . . Your country, your posterity [future generations] your God demands of you to ARM! ARM!! ARM!!!

Let the one universal rallying cry, from the Firth of Forth to the Land's End be EQUALITY OR DEATH.

(The *London Democrat*, 20 April 1839)

Source 1.63 *A moderate newspaper's comment*
Physical force is a thing not to be lightly had recourse to [used]; . . .

. . . Nothing but a simultaneous rising at the same hour all over the kingdom could give you a *chance* of success by arms – even that would give you but a slender chance, and that you *cannot* effect . . . Continue these acts of bucaneering folly, *and you and your children are slaves for ever.*

(The *Chartist*, 12 May 1839)

Source 1.64 *General Napier's warning*
Journal, December 1st – An anonymous letter come, with a Chartist plan. Poor creatures, their threats of attacks are miserable. With half a cartridge, and half a pike, with no money, no discipline, no skilful leaders, they would attack men with leaders, money and discipline, well armed, and having sixty rounds a man.

(W. Napier, *The Life and Opinions of General Sir Charles James Napier*, 1857, vol. 11, p. 93)

Moral force

Source 1.65 *A description of moral force from the Rules of the Leeds Radical Universal Suffrage Association*
The attainment of Universal Suffrage and the other main points of the Charter, by the use of every moral and lawful means, such as petitioning Parliament, procuring the return of Members of Parliament who will vote for Universal Suffrage and the other points of the Charter, publishing tracts, establishing reading rooms, holding public meetings for addresses and discussions, and giving public lectures on subjects connected with the politics of the country.

(*Northern Star*, 2 May 1840)

Source 1.66 *William Lovett – the main supporter of moral force*
The whole physical force agitation is harmful and injurious to the movement. Muskets are not what are wanted, but education and schooling of the working people. Stephens and O'Connor are shattering the movement . . . O'Connor wants to take everything by

storm, and to pass the Charter into law within a year. All this hurry and haste, this bluster and menace of armed opposition can only lead to . . . the destruction of Chartism.

(William Lovett, *Life and Struggles of William Lovett*, 1876 ed)

However another leading Chartist described moral force as 'trying to drive a nail with a feather'.

The 'Sacred Month'

Source 1.67 *The decision of the National Convention*
It is therefore the opinion of the National Convention that the people should work no longer after the 12th of August next, unless the power of voting for Members of Parliament to enable them to protect their labour and their rights is previously given and guaranteed to them.

(*The Charter*, 21 July 1839)

Source 1.68 *General Napier's view*
The Chartists say they will keep the sacred month. Egregious [remarkable] folly! They will do no such thing; the poor cannot do it; they must plunder, and then they will be hanged by the hundreds . . .

(Napier)

Source 1.69 *Feargus O'Connor's view*
If I thought you could test the value of labour by a month's holiday, I would say have it . . . But you know

– you all know – that the baker will not bake, the butcher will not kill, and the brewer will not brew; and then what becomes of the millions of starving human beings? . . . Make your necessary arrangements; have a three days' holiday instead of a month's strike and what you fail to effect by it, would have been equally lost by the month . . . but I never will, with a certainty of my own dinner, recommend a project which may cause millions to starve . . .

(*Northern Star*, 3 August 1839)

As expected the Charter was rejected by Parliament. The 'Sacred Month' got little support, and fizzled out in a few days. Some outbreaks of violence did occur, the most serious of which was at Newport in Wales:

Source 1.70 *The Newport Rising*
A company of the 45th Regiment was stationed at the Westgate Hotel, and thither the multitude marched, loudly cheering as they marched through the streets. Arrived in front of the Hotel, an attack was immediately commenced; . . . The soldiers were stationed at the windows, through which a number of the people began to fire . . . The soldiers . . . returned the fire . . . the consequence was, that in about twenty minutes ten of the Chartists were killed upon the spot, and about fifty others wounded.

(R. G. Gammage, *History of the Chartist Movement, 1837–1854*, 1894 ed., p. 162)

Source 1.71 **The Newport Rising**

The second petition and the 'Plug Plot'

The leaders of the Newport Rising were sentenced to death, later changed to transportation. In fact, by 1840, most Chartist leaders, including Lovett and O'Connor, were in prison. More work was available and Chartism lost its mass support for a time.

Unemployment, poverty and discontent returned in 1842. The Chartists presented another petition to Parliament, but it was again rejected. A wave of strikes spread throughout the manufacturing towns of northern England. Workers removed the plugs from the steam engines bringing the factories to a halt. The Chartists did not start this protest, but soon gave it their support.

Source 1.72 *Distress in Manchester*
Any man passing through the district and observing the condition of the people, will at once perceive the deep ... distress that prevails ... spreading discontent and misery where recently happiness and content were enjoyed. The picture which the manufacturing districts now present is absolutely frightful. Hungry and half-clothed men and women are stalking through the streets begging for bread.

(*Manchester Times*, 9 July 1842)

Source 1.73 *The 'Plug Plot'*
'The Plug Plot' of 1842, as it is still called in Lancashire, began in reduction of wages by the manufacturers. The people advanced at last, to a wild general strike, and drew the plugs from the steam boilers so as to stop the work at the mills, and thus render labour impossible. The first meeting where the resolution was passed 'that all labour should cease until the People's Charter became the law of the land' was held on the 7th of August ... In the course of a week, the resolution had been passed in nearly all the great towns of Lancashire, and tens of thousands had held up their hands in favour of it.

(Thomas Cooper, *Life of Thomas Cooper by Himself*, 1879)

Within a few weeks, hunger had forced many of the strikers back to work, and the strike collapsed.

The Chartist Land company

After 1842 employment prospects improved, especially with the demand for labourers to build the new railways. The Chartists' political aims had been rejected by Parliament again; and now some Chartists turned to other interests.

Feargus O'Connor set up the Chartist Land Company. Its aim was to buy land where new communities would be created. Workers would buy shares in the company, and once settled on the land, they would escape the horrors of the industrial towns and would lead peaceful, contented lives. O'Connor did his best to make the scheme popular, and five communities were set up; one of them was named O'Connorville. Unfortunately O'Connor knew nothing about farming or running a company, and by 1851 the scheme had collapsed.

Source 1.74 *O'Connor's reasons for the scheme*
The position we should wish man to occupy on THE LAND, is one of independence! To be there his own master! To have sufficient of surface in his occupation to occupy his labour hours, and to return him an adequate LIVING. To so occupy, that every improvement he made should be mainly his own, so that he might have every inducement to make improvements.

(*Northern Star*, 14 January 1843)

Source 1.75 *A view of O'Connor's ideas on farming*
Every acre was to yield on average such crops as no acre ever did yield except under the rarest combinations of favouring climate, consummate skill and unlimited manure – and then only occasionally. Every cow was to live for ever, was to give more milk than any save the most exceptional cow ever gave before, and was never to be dry. Every pig was to be a prime one, every goose to be a swan.

(*Edinburgh Review*)

Source 1.76 Snigs End, – a Chartist community in Gloucestershire

Source 1.77 *An open day at O'Connorville*

On arriving at O'Connorville, at twelve o'clock, we found a vast number of persons had preceded us by other routes . . . even from Yorkshire and Lancashire in the north; and from Exeter and Plymouth in the West . . .

On entering the gates, the band played 'The Chartist Land March' . . . The first object that met our view, was a huge tri-coloured banner floating, high above an immense chestnut tree, bearing the inscription, 'O'Connorville' . . .

(*Northern Star*, 22 August 1846)

Source 1.78 *The failure of the scheme – eviction from a Chartist settlement*

It was anticipated that these proceedings would be resisted in a formidable manner by the occupiers. Nothing of the kind, however, was attempted: each party left in a peaceful manner: many were in a very destitute [needy] condition, and exclaimed loudly against the scheme, which in the first instance, told such a plausible tale of the lasting benefits it would confer on the shareholders, but which now had reduced them to the necessity of returning from whence they came, with little or no means, and entirely ruined in their prospects.

(*Oxford Chronicle*, 23 November 1850, quoted in A. Briggs (ed.), *Chartist Studies*, Macmillan, 1959, p. 333)

The third petition

Hard times returned in 1847 and Chartism revived. The Chartists received further encouragement from the overthrow of the King of France. It was decided that another giant petition would be collected – but this time the Chartists would go to London with it. After a mass meeting at Kennington Common, the Chartists planned to march to Parliament with the petition and demand that the Charter be made law.

Source 1.79 *Revolution in France*

Heroic citizens [of Paris]. The thunder notes of your victory have sounded across the Channel awakening the sympathies and hopes of every lover of liberty . . . The fire that consumed the throne of the royal traitor and tyrant will kindle the torch of liberty in every country in Europe.

(*Northern Star*, 12 March 1848)

Source 1.80 *Government preparations*

The measures of Government, devised and personally worked by the Duke of Wellington, were on a large and complete scale . . . The Thames bridges were the main points of concentration; bodies of foot and horse police . . . being posted at their approaches on either side. In the immediate neighbourhood of each of them, within call, a strong force of military was kept ready for instant movement . . . Two regiments of the line were kept in hand at Millbank Penitentiary; 1200 infantry at Deptford Docks, and thirty pieces of heavy field ordnance at the Tower, all ready for transport by hired steamers, to any spot where serious business might threaten. At other places, also, bodies of troops were posted, out of sight, but within sudden command . . . and such places as the Bank of England were packed with troops and artillery, and strengthened with sandbag parapets on their walls . . .

In addition to the regular civil and military force, it is credibly estimated that at least 120 000 special constables were sworn and organized . . .

(The *Annual Register*, 1848)

Source 1.81 *The Prime Minister's account of the Kennington Common meeting*

About 12 000 or 15 000 persons met in good order. Feargus O'Connor, upon arriving upon the ground in a car, was ordered by Mr Mayne [the Commissioner of Police] to come and speak to him. He immediately left the car and came, looking pale and frightened, to Mr Mayne. Upon being told that the meeting would not be prevented, but that no procession would be allowed to pass the bridges, he expressed the utmost thanks, and begged to shake Mr Mayne by the hand. He then addressed the crowd, advising them to disperse, and after rebuking them for their folly he went off in a cab to the Home Office, where he repeated to Sir George Grey [the Home Secretary] his thanks, his fears, and his assurances that the crowd should disperse quietly. Sir George Grey said he had done very rightly, but that the force at the bridges should not be diminished.

Mr F. O'Connor – 'Not a man should be taken away. The Government have been quite right. I told the Convention that if they had been the Government they never would have allowed such a meeting.'

(Lord John Russell to Queen Victoria, 10 April 1848 in A. C. Benson and Viscount Esher, eds, *The Letters of Queen Victoria*, 1908, II, pp. 168–9)

Source 1.82 *A Chartist's account of the Kennington Common meeting*

I was standing near the van in which were the members of the Executive Council and many delegates of the National Convention, with the piled-up rolls of the petition, when I heard a cry of, 'They have got him!' And a wild rush was made towards the western side of the Common. Looking in that direction, I saw the giant form of Feargus O'Connor . . . towering above the throng, as he moved towards the road, accompanied by a courageous inspector of police.

Presently O'Connor was seen returning, and his reappearance was hailed with a tremendous shout. He mounted the van, and in a few words explained the state of affairs to the anxious throng. He had had an interview with Sir Richard Mayne at the Horns Tavern, and concessions had been made on both sides. The Government had consented to allow the meeting to be held without molestation, and the honourable member for Nottingham [O'Connor] had promised to use his influence with the masses for the purpose of inducing them to abandon the intended procession to the House of Commons with the petition . . .

(Thomas Frost, *Forty Years Recollections*,
Sampson Low, 1880, p. 140)

Source 1.83 The Chartist meeting on Kennington Common

Source 1.84 *Parliament's examination of the Petition* The Hon. Member for Nottingham [Mr F. O'Connor] stated on presenting the petition, that 5 706 000 names were attached to it; but upon the most careful examination . . . the number of signatures has been ascertained to be 1 975 496. It is further evident to your Committee that on numerous consecutive sheets the signatures are in one and the same handwriting. Your Committee also observed the names of distinguished individuals attached to the petition, who can scarcely be supposed to concur to its prayer; among which occurs the name of Her Majesty, as Victoria Rex, April 1st, F. M. Duke of Wellington, Sir Robert Peel, etc.

Your Committee have also observed . . . the insertion of numbers of names which are obviously fictitious, such as 'No Cheese', 'Pug Nose', 'Flat Nose'. There are others included, which your Committee do not hazard offending the House and the dignity and the decency of their own proceedings by reporting.

(Select Committee on Public Petitions, *Hansard*,
1849)

Using the Evidence

1. Read sources 1.54 and 1.55 closely. Which of the following statements best sums up these extracts?
   (a) The Reform Act was greatly welcomed by working people
   (b) The Reform Act made no difference to working people
   (c) The Reform Act made life worse for working people

2. Does source 1.56 prove or disprove your answer to question 1?

3. Compare sources 1.58 and 1.59. One of them is taken from a document to be presented to Parliament; the other is taken from a speech to a large Chartist meeting. Give your reasons for saying which is which.

4. Examine the Six Points of the Charter in source 1.60. The Chartists' main demand was Point One; so why did they want the other Five? Set your answer in a table like this:

   Point   *Reason*
   2. Secret ballot   So that people could vote fairly

5. Examine closely sources 1.61 to 1.69 which describe the three main options discussed by the Chartists in 1839 – physical force, moral force and a month's strike. Make rough notes describing the advantages and disadvantages of each. Then write a paragraph stating which one you would have advised them to use. You must give clear reasons from the extracts to support your choice.

6. Study source 1.70 and then look again at sources 1.61 to 1.64. Which of these views of physical force does source 1.70 support?

7. Using sources 1.74, 1.75, 1.76, 1.77 and 1.78, try to explain why someone might have decided to go to live in a Chartist settlement.

8. From source 1.79, explain why the government was taking such a serious view of the planned meeting.

9. Look at source 1.84. How might the publication of these details affect support for Chartism?

Coursework

Role of Individual

1. In this assignment you are going to try to assess the importance of Feargus O'Connor to the Chartist movement. Use these points to help you:
   What means did O'Connor have for spreading Chartist ideas, and how effective were they?
   Was he genuine in his support for the working class? E.g. see source 1.69.
   What really was his attitude to using physical force?
   Do you think his decisions at the Kennington Common Meeting (sources 1.80–83) were correct?
   Consider his part in the Chartist Land Plan. What did that scheme suggest firstly, that O'Connor was good at, and secondly, he was not good at?
   Was O'Connor an important working-class leader?

Causation

2. Why did Chartism fail? Answer these questions to help you:
   (a) How united was the movement?
   (b) How reliable were the leaders, e.g. O'Connor?
   (c) How consistent was the mass support for Chartism?
   (d) What was the attitude of Parliament and the authorities to it?

2 The Poor

Eventide (Hubert von Herkomer)

Poor People in Town and Country

There are still poor people in Britain today. But if you had lived in Britain between 1815 and 1851, you would have seen much more evidence of poverty. There were far more poor people then, who lived in conditions of poverty we can hardly imagine now. Middle- and upper-class people could live very comfortable lives, but many working people in the towns and the countryside lived on the edge of starvation. In fact, the government, made up of upper-class landowners – the only class represented in Parliament in 1815 – were unaware of the large numbers of poor people.

A changing Britain

In the years before 1815, great changes had taken place in Britain. The population was rapidly increasing. During the 'Industrial Revolution' many people had moved from the countryside to find work in the textile factories, ironworks and mines of the growing industrial areas – the Midlands and the north of England, the Central Lowlands of Scotland, and south Wales.

But although factories and mines provided work for hundreds of thousands of people, those who went to work in industrial towns often had to work for very low wages, and live in dreadful conditions.

Also, many factory workers were thrown out of work when there was a slump in trade, and orders for cloth fell. When he was unemployed, or if he was too old or sick to work, the factory worker and his family suffered great hardship. There was no scheme of social security provided by the government as there is today.

Source 2.1 Population Increase (in thousands)

Industrial towns	1801	1851
Glasgow	77	329
Bradford	13	104
Leeds	53	172
Manchester	70	303
Liverpool	82	376
Sheffield	46	135
Birmingham	71	233
London	957	2362

Poverty in the industrial towns

Source 2.2 Families were attracted from all parts for the benefit of employment, and obliged ... to crowd together into such dwellings as the neighbourhood afforded: often two families into one house; others into cellars ... eventually ... the proprietor ... would probably ... build a few cottages; these were often of the worst description: ... the prevailing consideration was not how to promote the health and comfort of the occupants, but how many cottages could be built upon the smallest space of ground and at the least possible cost.

('Report on the Sanitary Conditions of the Labouring Population', Lords Sessional Reports, 1842, vol. 26, p. 239)

Source 2.3 Back-to-back city slums in the nineteenth century

Source 2.4 The streets most densely populated by the humbler classes are a mass of filth where the direct rays of the sun never reach. In some of the courts I have noticed heaps of filth, amounting to 20 or 50 tons, which, when it rains, penetrate into some of the cellar dwellings. A few public necessaries have been built, but too few to serve the population . . .

Stagnant ditches may be seen in the vicinity of most of these houses . . . and long open sewers cross the public paths . . .

In numerous dwellings a whole family shares one room . . .

. . . Dense black clouds of smoke from manufacturing prevail to a great extent . . .'

(Dr D. B. Reid, 'Report on the Sanitary Conditions of Newcastle, Gateshead, North Shields, Sunderland, Durham and Carlisle', 1845)

The hand-loom weavers

Of all workers in industrial towns, hand-loom weavers and their families suffered the greatest hardship. Years before, when factories only spun thread, the hand-loom weavers were in great demand, and earned a very good living:

Source 2.5 Four days did the weaver work, for then four days was a week . . . and such a week to a skilled workman brought forty shillings. Sunday, Monday and Tuesday were of course jubilee. Lawn frills gorged freely from under the wrists of his fine blue, gilt-buttoned coat. He dusted his head with white flour on Sunday, smirked, and wore a cane. Walked in clean slippers on Monday. Tuesday heard him talk war bravado . . . and get drunk. Weaving commenced gradually on Wednesday . . .

(William Thom, *Rhymes and Recollections of a Handloom Weaver*, London, 1845, p. 9)

Source 2.6 Hand-loom weaver

But trade was reduced during the wars against France, and when more and more factories began to use power looms, there was less and less work for the hand-loom weavers, who rapidly went out of business.

Source 2.7 A very good hand-loom weaver will weave two pieces of cloth, each 24 yards long. A steam loom weaver . . . will in the same time weave 7 similar pieces . . . the work done in the steam factory containing 200 looms would, if done by handloom weavers, find employment and support for a population of more than 2000 persons.

(Richard Guest, *A Compendious History of the Cotton Manufacture*, 1823)

Source 2.8 Power looms in a factory

Source 2.9 A very great number of the weavers are unable to provide for themselves a sufficiency of the plainest and cheapest kind; that they are clothed in rags . . . that they have scarcely anything like furniture in their houses; that their beds and bedding are of the most wretched description, and that many of them sleep upon straw; that notwithstanding their want . . . they . . . have full employment; that their labour is excessive, not infrequently 16 hours a day . . .

('Report of Handloom Weavers Committee' *Parliamentary Papers*, 1835, p. xii)

Source 2.10 The Poor Man's Friend (*Punch*)

Source 2.11 No labourer can at present maintain himself, wife and two children on his earnings; they all have relief [help] from the parish . . . A very few years ago . . . labourers thought themselves disgraced by receiving aid [payments] from the parish, but this sense of shame is now totally extinguished.

(Sir Frederick Eden, *The State of the Poor in 1797*, vol. II, p. 137)

A farm labourer's cottage in the nineteenth century:

Source 2.12 The Cottage (*Punch* 1861)

THE COTTAGE.

Mr. Punch (to Landlord). "YOUR STABLE ARRANGEMENTS ARE EXCELLENT! SUPPOSE YOU TRY SOMETHING OF THE SORT HERE! EH

Poverty in the countryside

In the countryside, there was probably even more poverty than in the towns. Each one of the new 'enclosed' farms had been created from land previously worked by many farmers. There was a lot of unemployment because many farmers lost their land, and the 'enclosed' farms needed fewer labourers to work on them. Those labourers who kept their jobs had to work for very low wages. New machinery such as threshing machines was taking away some of the work done by labourers. After the Napoleonic Wars with France ended in 1815, there was a slump in agriculture and farm labourers became poorer still.

Source 2.13 The length is not above 15 feet, its width between 10 and 12 . . . The wall . . . has sunk at different parts, and seems bedewed with a cold sweat . . . You have to stoop for admission . . . there are but two rooms in the house – one below and the other above . . . Before you is a large but cheerless fireplace . . . with a few smouldering embers of a small wood fire, over which hangs a pot . . . At one corner stands a small rickety table, whilst scattered about are three old chairs . . . and a stool or two . . . Let us take a look at their sleeping accommodation . . . There is but one room, and yet we counted nine in the family! . . . The beds are large sacks, filled with chaff of oats . . . It not infrequently happens that the clothes worn by the parents in the daytime form the chief part of the covering of the children by night.

(P. E. Razzell and R. W. Wainwright (eds) *The Victorian Working Class*, 1973)

1. From source 2.1, say what was happening to the population of industrial towns in the first half of the nineteenth century.

2. From source 2.2, find words and phrases to show that most factory owners were not concerned with the welfare of their workers when they built houses for them. What is the main criticism here of such houses? (You can also see evidence of this in source 2.3.)

3. From source 2.4:
   (a) What did the houses lack compared to modern houses?
   (b) What dangers were there to the health of workers living in these houses?

4. Using the evidence in sources 2.2, 2.3, 2.4, say why disease spread so quickly in industrial towns.

5. List as many pieces of evidence as you can from source 2.5 to show how well off hand-loom weavers were before the coming of power looms.

6. From source 2.7, say why the use of power looms caused unemployment among hand-loom weavers. How do sources 2.6 and 2.8 help us understand why many hand-loom weavers were unemployed?

7. What evidence is there of the poverty of hand-loom weavers in source 2.9? What is surprising therefore in the last two lines of the extract?

8. Look at source 2.10.
   (a) What is there to show that this man lived in poverty?
   (b) Who was his 'friend'? Why is it described as the '*friend*' of the poor man?
   (c) What do you think was *Punch* magazine's reason for publishing this picture?

9. Look at sources 2.11 to 2.13.
   (a) How had farm labourers come to feel because they were so poor?
   (b) How could they live, if their earnings were too low to support them?
   (c) From source 2.12, find as many pieces of evidence as you can to show how poor the farm labourer's family was.
   (d) How do we know that Mr Punch regards the cottage as unfit to live in?
   (e) In source 2.13 what tells you the cottage was unhealthy to live in?
   (f) What evidence is there that the cottage was overcrowded?
   (g) Make a list of the few belongings of the labourer's family. How do the contents of the cottage compare with the contents of a house today?

Poor Relief in the Early Nineteenth Century

There was no single system of poor relief (helping the poor) in Britain at this time. Most kinds of poor relief were based on the country parish. Thomas Gilbert's Act of 1782 tried to ensure that only old and sick paupers (poor people) and orphans were kept in a workhouse; able bodied paupers were given an allowance of money (outdoor relief) to look after themselves. In the Roundsman system, paupers had to go round the parish looking for work. If they found a job, the parish would pay part of their wages, but this meant that the employer would pay as small a share as possible. In Scotland, the Presbyterian Church – the Kirk – regarded it as its duty to help the poor. It usually shared the cost of poor relief with town councils in the towns, and with landowners in the countryside.

Many people and governments in the early nineteenth century were influenced by Thomas Malthus' ideas on population growth and poor relief:

Source 2.14 The poor laws of England tend to depress the general condition of the poor . . . Their first obvious tendency is to increase population without increasing the food for its support. A poor man may marry with little or no prospect of being able to support a family . . .

. . . The labouring poor . . . seem always to live from hand to mouth . . . they seldom think of the future. Even when they have the opportunity of saving they seldom exercise it.; but all that is beyond their present necessities goes . . . to the ale-house. The poor-laws in England may therefore be said to diminish the . . . will to save, among the common people, and . . . weaken one of the strongest incentives to sobriety and industry, and consequently to happiness . . .

(Thomas Malthus, *Essay on Population*, 1798)

Thomas Malthus

The Speenhamland system

In 1795, the magistrates in the parish of Speenhamland in Berkshire thought they had found a solution to the problem of the poverty of landless labourers. They began a scheme by which labourers in need received a weekly payment based on the cost of living. This 'Speenhamland system' was widely copied in other parishes throughout the agricultural south of England. Instead of solving the problem, however, it actually made matters worse.

Source 2.15 Resolved unanimously,
That the present state of the Poor does require further assistance than has been generally given them.
Resolved,
. . . that they [that is, the magistrates] will . . . make the following calculations and allowances for the relief of all poor and industrious men and their families, who to the satisfaction of the Justices of their Parish, shall endeavour (as far as they can) for their own support and maintenance.

That is to say,
When the Gallon Loaf of Second Flour, weighing 8 lb. 11 ozs. [almost 4 kg] shall cost 1s [5p].
Then every poor and industrious man shall have for his own support 3s. weekly, either produced by his own or his family's labour, or an allowance from the poor rates, and for the support of his wife and every other of his family, 1s. 6d.
When the Gallon Loaf shall cost 1s. 4d.
Then every poor and industrious man shall have 4s. weekly for his own, and 1s. and 10d. for every other of his family.
And so on in proportion, as the price of bread rise or falls (that is to say) 3d. to the man, and 1d. to every other of the family, on every 1d. which the loaf rise above 1s.

By order of the Meeting,
W. BUDD, Deputy Clerk of the Peace.

(The *Reading Mercury*, 11 May 1795)

Source 2.16 This is part of a table published by the Speenhamland magistrates.

	Income should be for a Man	For a Single Woman	For a Man and his Wife	With one Child	With two Children
When the gallon loaf is 1s.0d.[5p]	3s.0d.[15p]	2s.0d.[10p]	4s.6d.[22½p]	6s.0d.[30p]	7s.6d.[37½p]
When " " 1s.1d.	3s.3d.	2s.1d.	4s.10d.	6s.5d.	8s.0d.
When " " 1s.2d.	3s.6d.	2s.2d.	5s.2d.	6s.10d.	8s.6d.
When " " 1s.3d.	3s.9d.	2s.3d.	5s.6d.	7s.3d.	9s.0d.
When " " 1s.4d.	4s.0d.	2s.4d.	5s.10d.	7s.8d.	9s.6d.

Here is part of an interview with Thomas Pearce, a Sussex labourer, in 1834. It clearly shows the effect of the Speenhamland system of poor relief on the labourers' attitude to work.

Source 2.17 'In your parish are there many able-bodied men upon the parish?'

'There are a great many men in our parish who like it better than being at work.'

'Why do they like it better?'

'They get the same money and don't do half so much work. They don't work like me; they be'ant at it so many hours, and they don't do so much work when they be at it; they're doing no good, and are only waiting for dinner time and night; they be'ant working, it's only waiting.'

'How have you managed to live without parish relief?'

'By working hard.'

'What do the paupers say to you?'

'They blame me for what I do. They say to me "What are you working for?" I say "For myself!" They say "You are only doing it to save the parish, and if you didn't do it, you would get the same as another man has, and would get the money for smoking your pipe and doing nothing." 'Tis a hard thing for a man like me.'

(*Report of the Poor Law Commission*, 1834)

--------------- **Using the Evidence** ---------------

1. Look at source 2.14. Which of the following statements correctly describe Thomas Malthus' ideas about poor relief, and which do not:
   (a) If you give poor relief payments to those in need, they will waste the money on enjoying themselves, without thinking of the future.
   (b) Poor people would not be grateful for poor relief payments.
   (c) Poor people who were supported by the parish would only marry and have children, which would increase the number of poor people.
   (d) If you help poor people, they would be more likely to find a job and improve their standard of living.

2. Would Malthus' ideas on population and poor relief be more likely or less likely to make governments want to give more help to poor people?

3. Look at source 2.15. Say what 2 things determined the amount of money an unemployed (or low-paid) labourer received on the Speenhamland scale.

4. From source 2.16 who received least, and who most, poor relief on the Speenhamland scale?

5. The Speenhamland magistrates were trying to create a fair system of poor relief. Say in your own words how the Speenhamland scale tried to be fair to the poor.

6. Look at source 2.17.
   (a) According to Thomas Pearce, why did many labourers not want to work?
   (b) What was the feeling of other labourers towards the hard-working Thomas Pearce? What did they mean by 'You are only doing it to save the parish'?
   (c) How might the attitude of other labourers eventually affect Thomas Pearce?
   (d) Look back to source 2.14. Quote words and phrases to show that when the Berkshire magistrates drew up the Speenhamland scale, they did *not intend* to discourage labourers from working.

7. Look at sources 2.14 to 2.17.

   (a) Why could an employer lower his labourers' wages, thinking he was causing them no harm?
   (b) What would happen to the cost of poor relief as the labourers wages fell?
   (c) Landowners paid the rates which paid for poor relief. Did it make sense for them to lower their labourers' wages?

Protesting Against Poverty

The 'Swing' riots, 1830–1

By 1830, British agriculture was in serious difficulties, despite the Corn Law of 1815 (see Chapter 1). Farmers reduced labourers' wages and many labourers were made unemployed. The situation was worst in the rural south and south-east of England, in counties such as Hampshire, Berkshire, Wiltshire, Kent and Norfolk. There, many labourers were receiving poor relief under the 'Speenhamland system'. In some places, magistrates actually reduced poor relief payments because of protests by landowning rate-payers. The result was riots by labourers throughout the south of England in 1830 and 1831. Most riots were directed at unpopular landowners who had reduced labourers' wages or were using the new threshing machines which were putting many labourers out of work.

The riots were supposed to be the work of a 'Captain Swing' whose name was signed on letters received by landowners and the authorities, who were greatly alarmed. The new Whig government, elected in 1830, wanted to suppress the riots as quickly as possible, and gave instructions to magistrates to take action against rioters and arrest as many as they could. In all, 1976 rioters were tried: 19 were executed, 505 were transported to convict settlements overseas, and 644 were sent to prison.

The 'Swing' riots did not achieve much relief in the hardship of agricultural labourers. Sometimes farmers did increase labourers' wages, and stopped using threshing machines, as a result of threats of violence. But generally, farm labourers continued to live in great poverty. However, the riots did draw the government's attention to the high level of poverty in the countryside, and showed that the 'Speenhamland system' of poor relief was not working.

The authorities' view

Source 2.18 SWING, EH! OUTRAGES IN KENT. Dover, October 6. – The county of Kent is in a very agitated state, on account of the organised system of stack-burning and machine-breaking ... the High Sheriff of the County lately attended one of their [i.e. the fire-raisers'] meetings ... one of them said 'We will destory the corn stacks ... this year. Next year we will have a turn with the parsons, and the third we will make war upon the Statesmen.' What will such a state of things end in? ... Anonymous letters, signed 'Swing', have been received ... the *Sheffield Courant*, in noticing the Belgium affair, very properly remarks, 'If we do not mistake the indications ... there are dangers nearer home, which our government may be too blind to see, but which, nevertheless, threaten Europe with terrible, sweeping, and extensive convulsions ...'

(From a leaflet published by Henry Hetherington, *Home Office papers* 40/25, 1830)

Source 2.19 *The Duke of Wellington's advice*
I induced the magistrates to put themselves on horseback, each at the head of his own servants and retainers, grooms, huntsmen, gamekeepers, armed with horsewhips, pistols, fowling-pieces ... and to attack ... these mobs, disperse them, and take and put in confinement those who could not escape. This was done in a spirited manner ... and it is astonishing how soon the country was tranquillised, and that in the best way, by the activity and spirit of the gentlemen.

(In E. J. Hobsbawm and G. Rudé, *Captain Swing*, Lawrence and Wishart, 1970, p. 255)

In support of the labourers

Source 2.20
The labourers here look as if they were half-starved ... I really am ashamed to ride a fat horse, to have a full belly, and to have a clean shirt upon my back when I look at those wretched countrymen of mine; while I actually see them reeling with weakness; when I see their poor faces present me with nothing but skin and bone.

(William Cobbett, *Rural Rides*, 1831)

The Times newspaper commented on what happened in most outbreaks of violence:

Source 2.21 ... There is no ground for concluding that there has been any extensive concert [plot] amongst them ... in many places their proceedings have been managed with astonishing coolness and regularity. The farmers have notice to meet the men: a deputation of two or more of the latter produce a written statement, well drawn up, which the farmers are required to sign ... The farmers ... agree to the demands they made: that is, they were not mad enough to refuse requests which they could not demonstrate to be unreasonable in themselves, and which were urged by three hundred or four hundred men, after a barn or two had been fired ...

(*The Times*, November 7 1830)

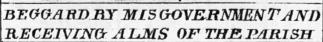

Source 2.22
Downfall of an
unemployed
labourer (Mansell
Collection)

Using the Evidence

1. Look at sources 2.18 and 2.19. According to these sources:
   (a) What crimes had farm labourers committed during the 'Swing' riots?
   (b) Which class of people was the violence aimed at?
   (c) What were the authorities afraid of? (The 'Belgium affair' in source 2.18 refers to the Belgian people rebelling against what they thought was an unfair Dutch government in 1830.)
   (d) Which class of people did the Duke of Wellington admire, in source 2.19?
   (e) The Duke was Prime Minister of the Tory government from 1828 to 1830, until the beginning of the 'Swing' riots. Would the Duke have agreed with the handling of the riots by the Whig government after 1830?

Source 2.23 Cartoon on the 'Swing' riots

2. Look at sources 2.20 and 2.21.
   (a) What good reason does William Cobbett give for the labourers' actions during the 'Swing' riots?
   (b) Quote three phrases from *The Times* source 2.21 to show that in many cases, the labourers acted in a responsible manner.
   (c) Why does *The Times* say that farmers sometimes agreed to labourers' demands? Find *two* reasons for this – one which suggests that that farmers agreed of their own free will, and one which suggests that they sometimes did not have much choice.

3. Look at source 2.23.
   (a) What evidence is there of 'Swing' violence? Who is being threatened?
   (b) Write out, *in your own words*, the two different responses to the 'Swing' riots put forward by the two men on the right of the picture. Which might have agreed with the Duke of Wellington, and which with the Radicals in Chapter 1. Which point of view do you think the cartoonist agreed with? Give reasons for your answer.

Coursework

Empathy

Tell the story in source 2.22 from the point of view of an unemployed labourer
or
From the point of view of a landowner who had suffered during the 'Swing' riots.

The Government and the Problem of Poverty

The 'Swing' riots had clearly shown the government that it had to try to deal with the problem of poverty, especially in the countryside. After the struggle for the Parliamentary Reform Act of 1832, the Whig government appointed a Royal Commission to study the existing methods of poor relief, and to make suggestions for improvements. The Poor Law Commissioners included such well-known men as Edwin Chadwick, a Manchester lawyer, and Nassau Senior, a leading economist and Professor at Oxford University. Chadwick's belief in ruthless efficiency dominated the Report of the Poor Law Commissioners.

The Report of the Poor Law Commissioners – outdoor relief

The Commissioners were especially concerned with payments made to the able-bodied poor under the Speenhamland system:

Source 2.24 It is true, that by the last Parliamentary return [that for the year ending 25 March 1832] the total amount of the money expended for the relief of the poor, [was] higher than for any year since the year 1820. . .

They had also noticed:

Source 2.25 . . . the increasing anxiety of the principal rate-payers, as their burden becomes more oppressive, to shift it in some way.

(*Poor Law Report*, 1834, p. 54)

In fact, the Commissioners had made up their minds even before they began their investigation. Their conclusion about 'outdoor relief' like the Speenhamland system was:

Source 2.26 Every penny bestowed that tends to render the position of the pauper more eligible [desirable] than that of the independent labourer, is a bounty [payment] on indolence and vice.

(*Poor Law Report*, 1834)

The Report of the Poor Law Commissioners – indoor relief

The Commissioners wanted to abolish the system of 'outdoor' relief and in its place, introduce a cheaper system of 'indoor' relief. The aim was to provide useful work for the able-bodied poor in workhouses. The

Edwin Chadwick

Commissioners intended separate types of workhouses for different types of poor people, but in practice this did not usually happen.

The government acted quickly, and included the proposals of the Poor Law Commissioners in the Poor Law Amendment Act of 1834. Poor relief on the lines of the Speenhamland system was to be ended, and workhouses were to be set up for the poor. Parishes were to be grouped into Poor Law 'Unions' which would organise workhouses in their Union areas.

A Central Poor Law Department in London, with Edwin Chadwick as its secretary, was to supervise the working of the new Poor Law and direct its operation from London.

The Commissioners' recommendations for workhouses

Source 2.27 The chief specific measures which we recommended are:
First. . . . all relief whatever to able-bodied persons or to their families otherwise than in well-regulated workhouses, . . . shall be declared unlawful, and shall cease . . .

At least four classes are necessary: (1) The aged and really impotent; (2) The children; (3) The able-bodied females; (4) The able-bodied males. Of whom we trust that the two latter will be the least numerous classes . . . and the requisite superintendence may be better obtained in separate buildings than under a single roof.

(*Poor Law Report*, 1834, pp. 262, 306–7)

Exceptions to having to enter a workhouse

Source 2.28
1. Where such person shall require relief on account of sudden and urgent necessity.
2. Where such person shall require relief on account of any sickness, accident, or bodily or mental infirmity. . .
3. Where such person being a widow, shall be in the first six months of widowhood.

(Poor Law Amendment Act, 1834)

Boards of Guardians

Source 2.29 XXXVII . . . where any Parishes shall be united . . . for the Relief of the Poor, a Board of Guardians of the Poor for such Union shall be constituted and chosen, and the Workhouse or Workhouses of such Union shall be administered, by such Board of Guardians; and the Guardians shall be elected by the Ratepayers.

(Poor Law Amendment Act, 1834)

Life in the workhouse

Workhouses were first set up gradually in the agricultural south of England. There were so many poor people, however, that it was impossible to stop the payment of 'outdoor' relief altogether.

Some workhouses were run efficiently, and as humanely as possible, but in general, life in the workhouse was very harsh. It was the treatment of paupers in the worst workhouses which received the most attention. There were many workhouse rules which caused great distress. In some workhouses, meals had to be eaten in silence; inmates could only receive visitors in the presence of a workhouse official; permission to leave the workhouse was sometimes only given if the inmate was going to church. Also, all types of paupers were usually kept in the same workhouse, although this was not intended by the Commissioners. For breaking workhouse rules, a pauper could be kept in solitary confinement, or his allowance of food reduced.

Source 2.30 Fulham and Hammersmith Workhouse, London

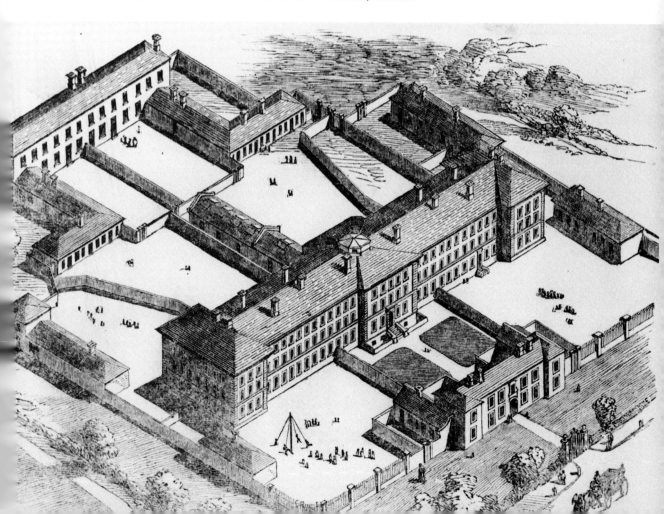

Source 2.31 *Division of families*

Art. 9. The paupers, so far as the workhouse admits thereof, shall be classed as follows. . . .

Class 1. Men infirm through age or any other cause.

Class 2. Able-bodied men, and youths above the age of 15 years.

Class 3. Boys above the age of 7 years, and under that of 15.

Class 4. Women infirm through age or any other cause.

Class 5. Able-bodied women, and girls above the age of 15.

Class 6. Girls above the age of 7 years, and under that of 15.

Class 7. Children under 7 years of age.

To each class shall be assigned that ward or separate building and yard which may be best fitted for the reception of such class, and each class of paupers shall remain therein, without communication with those of any other class.

(Workhouse rules drawn up by the Commissioners; *First Report of the Poor Law Commissioners*, 1835)

Source 2.33 WORKHOUSE (Rules of Conduct)

Any Pauper who shall neglect to observe such of the regulations herein contained as are applicable to and binding on him:

Or who shall make any noise when silence is ordered to be kept;

Or shall use obscene or profane language; . . .

Or shall refuse or neglect to work, after having been required to do so; . . .

Or shall play at cards or other games of chance; . . .
Shall be deemed DISORDERLY.

Any pauper who shall within seven days, repeat any one or commit more than one of the offences specified . . .

Or shall by word or deed insult or revile the master or matron, or any other officer of the workhouse, or any of the Guardians; . . .

Or shall be drunk; . . .

Or shall wilfully disturb the other inmates . . .
Shall be deemed REFRACTORY.

(Poor Law Commission, *Seventh Annual Report*, 1841)

Source 2.32 A Women's Ward in a Workhouse in the 1840s

STOW UNION.

DIETARY

FOR ABLE-BODIED MEN AND WOMEN.

		BREAKFAST		DINNER					SUPPER	
		Bread.	Gruel.	Meat pudding with Vegetables.	Suet pudding with Vegetables.	Bread.	Cheese.	Broth.	Bread.	Cheese.
		oz.	Pints.	oz.	oz.	oz.	oz.	Pints.	oz.	oz.
SUNDAY	Men	6	1½			8	1		6	1
	Women	5	1½			7	1		5	1
MONDAY	Men	6	1½	16					6	1
	Women	5	1½	10					5	1
TUESDAY	Men	6	1½			8	1		6	1
	Women	5	1½			7	1		5	1
WEDNESDAY,	Men	6	1½		16				6	1
	Women	5	1½		12				5	1
THURSDAY . . .	Men	6	1½			8	1		6	1
	Women	5	1½			7	1		5	1
FRIDAY	Men	6	1½	16					6	1
	Women	5	1½	12					5	1
SATURDAY . . .	Men	6	1½			8		1½	6	1
	Women	5	1½			7		1½	5	1

Old People, of Sixty Years of Age, and upwards, to be allowed 1 oz. of Tea, 5 oz. of Butter, and 7 oz. of Sugar per Week, in lieu of Gruel, for Breakfast.

Children under nine Years to be dieted at discretion; above Nine years to be allowed the same quantities as Women.

Sick to be dieted as directed by the Medical Officer.

[Woolby, Printer, Stowmarket.]

Source 2.34 The paupers' food

Source 2.35 The Old, Disabled and Mentally Ill in the Same Ward of a Workhouse

Source 2.36 *The scandal over conditions in Andover Union*
Evidence of Charles Lewis, labourer

[Mr. Wakely] What work were you employed about when you were in the workhouse? *I was employed breaking bones.*

Were other men engaged in the same work? – *Yes.*
Was that the only employment you had? – *That was the only employment I had at the time I was there.*

During the time you were so employed, did you ever see any men gnaw anything or eat anything from these bones? – *I have seen them eat marrow out of the bones.*

Did they state why they did it? – *I really believe they were hungry.*
Did you see any of the men gnaw the meat from the bones? – *Yes.*
Did they use to steal the bones and hide them away? – *Yes.*

(*Report from the Select Committee on the Andover Union*, 1846, p. 104)

The Rev. J. R. Stephens

Richard Oastler

Support for the new Poor Law

Many people supported the new Poor Law, and approved of the way in which the cost of looking after the poor was kept down. They included both the main political parties, the Tories and Whigs, the landowning upper class, and even many middle-class people.

Source 2.37 At a meeting of the Board of Guardians held at Highworth, on Wednesday the 11th of January, 1837, the following Resolutions were moved, seconded, and carried unanimously:

That the Board regard with . . . satisfaction the working of the Poor Law Amendment Act, during the twelve months it has been in operation in this Union of sixteen parishes, and 12 611 population.

That the . . . savings of the ratepayers, since the formation of the Union, as compared with the average expenditure of the three preceding years, is upwards of 54 per cent per annum.

That this large reduction has not been accomplished by causing privation to the aged or infirm, or the really . . . deserving poor, but by economy in the general management . . . and this . . . saving is also attended with decided symptoms of returning industry among the labouring poor . . .

Signed by order of the Board,

A. S. Crowdy, Clerk of the Union.

(Third Annual Report of the Poor Law Commissioners, pp. 182–3)

Source 2.38 Persons who could never be made to work before have become good labourers . . . there is a disposition to be more orderly and well-behaved . . . I may venture to say that the measure is working very satisfactorily . . . that the workhouse is held in great dread. . .

(*Second Annual Report of the Poor Law Commissioners*, p. 31. Evidence of the Chairman of the Market Harborough Union)

Opposition to the new Poor Law

From 1837, workhouses began to be set up in the Midlands and the north of England – areas which were much more industrial than the south. Though the workhouses had been hated by the poor in the south, it was in the north that most of the opposition to the new Poor Law arose. Large numbers of factory workers and hand-loom weavers were used to being unemployed at regular intervals when trade was bad and fewer workers were needed. For the workers of the north, the new Poor Law meant long and regular periods in a workhouse, instead of on 'outdoor' relief.

There was tremendous opposition to the workhouses, or 'Bastilles' as they were nicknamed after the infamous French prison destroyed during the French Revolution. It came not only from the poor and unemployed, but

also from such well-known men as the Todmorden factory owner John Fielden, the Radical Richard Oastler and the Rev. J. R. Stephens. Anti-Poor Law Associations were founded in the north of England, the best known being in Huddersfield, supported by Richard Oastler. Attacks on 'Bastilles' began to take place, such as the one at Stockport in 1842.

Source 2.39 *The Nottingham Guardians' failure to operate the workhouse system*

. . . it soon became evident that a necessity would speedily arise for relieving more persons than could be provided for within the walls of the workhouses, and, . . . we felt it to be our duty to authorise . . . the Guardians that the rule which prohibited them from giving relief to able-bodied male persons except in the workhouse should be suspended whenever they should find the pressure [caused] a necessity for so doing. Preparation was thus made for placing the Guardians in a situation to meet the whole difficulty . . . of affording the necessary relief to such destitute persons as might be unable to maintain themselves when thrown out of work.

(*Third Annual Report of the Poor Law Commissioners,* 1837, *Parliamentary Papers,* 1837, xxxi)

Source 2.40   The attack on Stockport Workhouse

Source 2.41   *The Rev. J. R. Stephens' case against workhouses*

The people were not going to stand this, and he would say, that sooner than wife and husband, and father and son, should be sundered and dungeoned, and fed on 'skillee', – sooner than wife or daughter should wear the prison dress – sooner than that – Newcastle ought to be, and should be – one blaze of fire, with only one way to put it out, and that with the blood of all who supported this abominable measure . . .

(Extract from a speech by the Rev. J. R. Stephens on the New Poor Law, January 1838; in R. G. Gammage, *History of the Chartist Movement,* 1854, pp. 64–5)

Source 2.42   *John Fielden, the Todmorden factory owner, trying to make the new Poor Law unworkable*

In Todmorden Union, immediately on the introduction of the new system, an attempt was made by the partners of one manufactory . . . to prevent the peaceable operation of the law, by throwing the whole of their work-people at once out of employment, and closing their works. . .

On the 16th November last two constables from Halifax, who were employed in executing a warrant of distress upon the overseer of Langfield, were violently assaulted and overpowered by a concourse of persons, the first assembling of which was accompanied by the ringing of a bell in one of Messrs. Fielden's factories, from which a large number of work-people issued, and took part in the riot which ensued . .

Such was the state of excitement and alarm occasioned by these unfortunate proceedings that the magistrates ... deemed it expedient on two occasions to call out a military force of the constables while engaged in making prisoners of some of the workmen in Messrs. Fielden's mills. It has also appeared essential to the security of the neighbourhood that a combined force of infantry and cavalry should be stationed at Todmorden for the present.

(*Fifth Annual Report of the Poor Law Commissioners,* 1839, pp. 31–4)

As well as taking part in sometimes violent protests against the new Poor Law, working-class labourers, the unemployed and poor expressed their discontent with the workhouse system in popular songs, often printed on sheets called broadsides. These circulated amongst the working class and poor, and provided a working-class view of the issues of the day (see Source 2.44).

This cartoon shows how many people felt about the new Poor Law compared to the old methods of 'outdoor' relief, such as the Speenhamland system:

Source 2.43 The Poor Laws – As they were, As they are

Source 2.44 *The new starvation law examined*
. . .

When a man and his wife for sixty long years
Have toiled together through troubles and fears,
And brought up a family with prudence and care,
To be sent to the Bastile it's very unfair.

And in the Bastile each woman and man
Is parted asunder, – is this a good plan?
A word of sweet comfort they cannot express,
For unto each other they ne'er have access.

To give them hard labour, it is understood
In handmills the grain they must grind for their feed.
Like men in a prison they work them in gangs,
With turning and twisting it fills them with pangs.

I'll give you an insight of their regulations,
Which they put in force in these situations,
They've school, chapel, and prison all under a roof,
And the governor's house stands a little aloof.

The master instructs them the law to obey,
The governor minds it's all work and no play,
And as for religion the parson doth teach
That he knows the gospel, – no other must preach.

Ye hard-working men, wherever you be,
I'd have you watch closely these men, d'ye see;
I think they're contriving, the country all ŏ'er,
To see what's the worst they can do to the poor.

(From a Bradford broadsheet probably published in
the years just after the new Poor Law was
introduced.)

The Poor Law in the 1840s

Such tremendous opposition made it difficult for
the Poor Law Commissioners to properly organise the working of the new Poor Law. In
place of the Poor Law Commissioners, the
government established a Poor Law Board in
1847, headed by a member of the government,
and responsible to Parliament for the working of
the Poor Law. But the government continued to
believe that the real cause of poverty was
idleness, and not unemployment and low wages.
So the workhouse system continued, still hated
and opposed by many in Britain.

In his book in 1852, Robert Paisley found
that Britain treated its poor much worse than
other countries looked after their own poor
people:

Source 2.45 The Workhouse as now organised is a
reproach and disgrace peculiar to England; nothing
corresponding to it is to be found throughout the
whole of the Continent of Europe. In France, the
medical patients of our Workhouses would be found
in 'hospitaux'; the infirm aged poor would be in
'hospices'; and the blind, the idiot, the lunatic, the
bastard child and the vagrant would similarly be
placed in an appropriate but separate establishment
. . . It is at once equally shocking to every principle
of reason and every feeling of humanity that all these
varied forms of wretchedness should thus be
crowded together into one common abode; . . .

(Robert Paisley, *Pauperism and Poor Laws*, 1852)

Working-class opposition to the new Poor
Law was so great that, when those who opposed
the Poor Law turned also to supporting the
Chartist movement, Chartism was turned from
an unimportant protest group into a mass
movement (see Chapter 1).

Using the Evidence

1. (a) Here are 4 possible reasons why the Poor Law Commissioners recommended
changes in methods of poor relief:
   (i) Concern for the suffering of poor people.
   (ii) Rate-payers' protests at the rising cost of poor relief.
   (iii) Fear of riots against poverty leading to revolution in Britain.
   (iv) Outdoor relief (like the Speenhamland system) was discouraging
   labourers from working.
   Look at sources 2.24, 2.25 and 2.26 in this section, and source 2.18 in the
   section on the 'Swing' riots. Quote phrases to show each of the four reasons.
   (b) From all the evidence available, which reasons seemed more important, and
   which less important, to the Poor Law Commissioners?

---

2. Look at sources 2.27, 2.28 and 2.29.
   (a) Which people were forced to accept 'indoor' relief (enter a workhouse) and which people could still receive 'outdoor' relief (like the Speenhamland system), by the 1834 Poor Law Amendment Act?
   (b) (i) What was required by the new Poor Law which a Poor Law Union (group of parishes) could afford, but a single parish could not?
      (ii) Which people elected the Poor Law Guardians? What would have been the main concern of these electors (and therefore of the Guardians) in running the new Poor Law? (If needed, look back to source 2.25).

3. Look at source 2.30. What can you see in the design of the workhouse to show that different groups of people – the old, sick, children etc. – could have been kept apart in it?

4. In source 2.31, the Poor Law Commissioners laid down how people living in a workhouse should be divided. What would happen to a pauper family when they entered the workhouse? How would you expect them to feel at this treatment?

5. Look at source 2.35. Were the Commissioners' rules carried out? What was wrong with keeping these people, who were poor for very different reasons, together?

6. Workhouse life has been compared to being in prison. Find evidence from each of the sources 2.30 to 2.34, and from the 'Life in the workhouse' section in general, to show that in some ways this was true.

7. From source 2.36, find out what was the 'scandal' in the workhouse in Andover Union.

8. Look at source 2.37.
   (a) What is the main reason the Board of Guardians at Highworth gave for supporting the new Poor Law?
   (b) Look back to p. 44. In what way did the Guardians at Highworth and the Poor Law Commissioners agree?

9. Look at source 2.38. Why did most of the upper and middle classes want the poor to 'dread' the workhouse? Did the Chairman at Market Harborough seem to be concerned at the feelings of poor people?

10. Look at source 2.39.
    (a) What kind of poor relief were the Nottingham Guardians proposing in addition to workhouses?
    (b) Why were they recommending this? Was it out of concern for the poor?

11. Does source 2.40 suggest opposition to the new Poor Law threatened 'the security of the neighbourhood'? Whose side is the artist on?

12. What warning did the Rev. J. R. Stephens give in source 2.41 if the new Poor Law was to be carried out?

13. Describe in your words the violence mentioned in source 2.42. What was it aimed at preventing? Was it aimed against 'the security of the neighbourhood'?

14. Look at source 2.43.
    (a) What contrast does the artist make between the old Poor Law (e.g. the Speenhamland system) and the new Poor Law of 1834?
    (b) Were people as well off under the Speenhamland system as the cartoonist makes out? What might be his reason for pretending they were?

15. Look at source 2.44.
    (a) Why does the writer call the workhouse a Bastile (Bastille)?
    (b) List the writer's criticisms of life in a workhouse in each of the verses 2 to 5.
    (c) Would the government and the Boards of Guardians agree with the view put

forward in the last two lines? What would working people and the unemployed think?

16. Look at Robert Paisley's criticisms of the workhouse system in source 2.45. How do they compare with the Poor Law Commissioners' original suggestions in 1834? Why is he so critical of the workhouse system in Britain?

Coursework

Motivation

1. Your evidence shows that life in a workhouse was usually unpleasant, and often very cruel. Why did the Poor Law Commissioners *deliberately* lay down such a strict and unpleasant life for paupers in a workhouse? (Think of the only way a poor person could avoid being confined in a workhouse.) Who were the Poor Law Commissioners and the government blaming when a family fell into poverty?

Causation

2. What were the *real* causes of poverty? (If needed, look back to Poor People in Town and Country earlier in this chapter.)

Empathy

3. Imagine you were one of a pauper family living in the late 1830s or 1840s. Explain why your family became poor and describe how you were treated when you were forced to enter a workhouse. State clearly how you felt about your treatment, and say why you thought it was unfair to treat poor people in this way.

4. Imagine you were one of the Poor Law Commissioners reporting to the government in 1840 on the working of the new Poor Law. What would you have said in favour of the Poor Law, and about the problems in carrying it out?

Similarity/Difference

5. Copy the table into your notebook. Then enter each of the phrases under the headings to which they apply.

SPEENHAMLAND SYSTEM	THE NEW POOR LAW OF 1834

'Indoor relief'
'Outdoor relief'
controlled by local magistrates
centrally controlled by the government
cheaper to operate
cost tied to the price of bread
unpopular with poor people
welcomed by rate-payers
expensive if the numbers of poor people increased rapidly
tried to discourage poor people from accepting help
discouraged some low-paid labourers from working
split up families
allowed families to stay together
made people suffer for being poor
was intended to be a humane way of helping poor people

Source 3.25 *A hewer's work*

No. 3, George Reid, 16 years old, coal hewer:

I pick the coal at the wall-face, and seldom do other work; have done so for six years; the seam is 26 inches [66 cm] high, and when I pick I am obliged to twist myself up: the men who work on this seam lie on their broadsides.

. . . it is horrible sore work; none ever come up to meals. Pieces of bread are taken down; boys and girls sometimes drink the water below . . .

. . . have often been hurt; was off idle a short bit ago, the pick having torn my flesh while ascending the shaft . . .

(Children's Employment Commission, *Report on the Collieries and Iron Works in the East of Scotland*, 1842, vol. II, p. 436)

Source 3.26 *A drawer's work*

No. 1 Janet Cumming, 11 years old, bears coals:
Works with father; has done so for two years . . .

I carry the large bits of coal from the wall-face to the pit bottom, and the small pieces called chows, in a creel; the weight is usually a hundredweight . . . it is some work to carry; it takes three journies to fill a tub of 4 cwt. [200 kg] . . . The roof is very low; I have to bend my back and legs, and the water comes frequently up to the calves of my legs; has no liking for the work; father makes me like it

(Children's Employment Commission, *Report on the Collieries and Iron Works in the East of Scotland*, 1842, vol. ii p. 436)

Source 3.27 A drawer

Source 3.28 Trapper at work

Source 3.29 *A mines inspector's report on trappers*
The children that excite the greatest pity are those who stand behind the doors to open and shut them: they are called trappers, who in the darkness, solitude and stillness as of night, eke out a miserable existence for the smallest of wages. I can never forget the first unfortunate creature that I met with: it was a boy of about eight years old, who looked at me as I passed with an expression the most abject and idiotic – like a thing, a creeping thing, peculiar to the place. On approaching and speaking to him he shrank trembling and frightened into a corner.

(*Parliamentary Papers*, 1842, vol. XV, p. 72)

Source 3.30   Women bearers

Source 3.31   *Reports on the health and safety of mine workers*

i) 20. That one of the most frequent causes of accidents in these mines is the want of superintendence [careful watching] by overlookers . . . to see to the security of machinery for letting down and bringing up the workpeople . . . the quantity of noxious gas . . . the places into which it is safe or unsafe to go with a naked lighted candle, and the security of the proppings to uphold the roof, etc.

(Children's Employment Commission (Mines), *Parliamentary Papers*, 1842, vol. XV, pp. 257–8)

ii) The collier population is subject to a peculiar disease which is vulgarly called the black-spit . . . It is a wasting of the lungs occasioned, as is supposed, by the inhaling of the coal-dust while working, and the expectoration [spit] is as black as the coal-dust itself. Many strong men are cut off by it before they reach the age of forty . . . they drop prematurely into the grave, between the ages of forty and sixty . . .

(*New Statistical Account*, Newton, Edinburghshire, 1840)

iii) 26. . . . in the thin seam mines, more especially, the limbs become crippled and the body distorted . . . the muscular powers give way . . . the workpeople are incapable of following their occupation, at an earlier period of life than is common in other branches of industry. 27. . . . and each generation of this class of the population is commonly extinct soon after fifty.

(Children's Employment Commission (Mines), *Parliamentary Papers*, 1842, vol. XV, pp. 258–9)

Source 3.32   *The Collier Lass – A 'Broadside'*
My name's Polly Parker, I come o'er from Worsley.
My father and mother work in the coal mine.
Our family's large, we have got seven children,
So I am obliged to work in the same mine. . . .

By the greatest of dangers each day I'm
  surrounded.
I hang in the air like a rope or a chain.
The mine may fall in, I may be killed or wounded,
May perish by damp or the fire of the train.

And what would you do if it were not for our
  labour?
In wretched starvation your days you would pass,
While we could provide you with life's greatest
  blessing.
Then do not despise the poor collier lass.

All the day long you may say we are buried,
Deprived of the light and the warmth of the sun.
And often at night from our bed we are hurried;
The water is in, and barefoot we run.

And though we go ragged and black are our faces,
As kind and as free as the best we'll be found,
And our hearts are as kind as your lords in fine
  places.
Although we're poor colliers who work underground.

(Broadside printed by Harkness, Preston, Madden Collection, Cambridge University Library)

1. Use sources 3.11 to 3.18 to help you construct a table to outline what it was like to work in a cotton mill in the early nineteenth century.

Hours of work per day	
Age of child workers	
Dangers to health	
Bad treatment by employers	
Unfair rules	

2. Here are the sources of 3.11, 3.14, 3.15, 3.16, 3.17. Which do you think might have exaggerated how bad factory working conditions actually were, and which do you think might be accepted as being unbiased? Give reasons for your answers.
   3.11 – a doctor who worked among the poor in Stockport, Peter Gaskell
   3.14 – a report ordered by Parliament on the health of the labouring people of Britain
   3.15 – from a book *Stubborn Facts from the Factories*, by a factory worker, James Leech
   3.16 – from the report of a committee ordered by Parliament to investigate the conditions children worked in
   3.17 – from a book about the life of an orphan apprenticed to a factory owner.

3. Does source 3.18, the Mill Children, suggest working conditions were bad or not? Give a reason for your answer.

4. Say what harm would come to a family if the children did not work in factories, according to source 3.21. Adults' wages for factory work were usually low. What truth was there in W. Cooke Taylor's argument?

5. Does Senior's description of factory work in source 3.22 agree with the evidence in the Working in the Factories section? (sources 3.11–3.18, pp. 59–61) Who would be helped most, if the government agreed with Senior, and did not shorten factory hours?

6. Samuel Smiles (source 3.23) said that government laws to shorten factory hours would not help working people. Would factory workers agree?

7. Using sources 3.24 to 3.30, describe the work of the different mine workers, and say what were the hardships and dangers of each job: hewer, drawer, trapper, bearer.

8. The Commissioners who investigated conditions in the mines reported in 1842, using pictures like 3.24, 3.27, 3.28 and 3.30, as well as written reports. How would the use of pictures like these help the cause of those people who supported improvements in the mines?

9. What were the main causes of illness and death among mine workers? Find 3 causes in source 3.31 (i), 1 cause in 3.31 (ii) and 1 more in 3.31 (iii).

10. Look at source 3.32 'The Collier Lass'.
    (a) What reason does Polly Parker give for all her family having to work in the mine?
    (b) What dangers of mine work does she mention?
    (c) Find words and phrases to show that many people had a low opinion of mine workers. Why do you think they felt like this? Were they right to feel like this? (Consider how important coal was to industry at this time.)

(d) Find words and phrases to show that Polly Parker (and many other mine workers) were *proud* of doing such a difficult and dangerous job and did not feel inferior to other people.

--- Coursework ---

Empathy

1. Write a paragraph to say how a child worker would feel about working at New Lanark instead of working in most other factories.

2. Sum up the arguments *for* and *against* Parliament passing laws to improve working conditions in factories.

3. Write a report to the Commissioners who were investigating conditions in the mines from 1840 to 1842. Quote interviews you have had with mine workers, and give your impressions and feelings on what you have seen in the mines. Make suggestions for improvements you would like to see carried out.

The Churches and Social Conditions

How were the bad social conditions suffered by so many working people to be improved? Governments at the time mainly represented the landowning upper class. Even after the Parliamentary Reform Act of 1832 (see Chapter 1) there were few middle-class and no working-class Members of Parliament to put forward arguments for improving social conditions. In any case, as we have seen, most governments believed in *laissez-faire* and were reluctant to intervene in the question of working conditions.

The Christian churches might have played an important part in helping those in need, and in bringing the appalling social conditions to the attention of the government. In fact, the Church of Scotland did take some responsibility for helping the poor (see Chapter 2). But the Church of England showed little concern about social conditions. Its 'respectable' middle-class congregations were not those in most need. Many churchmen felt that poverty, and bad living and working conditions were unavoidable and simply had to be suffered.

Source 3.33 *Church attendance*
We look . . . every Sunday, at our well-filled churches, and we forget . . . in the presence of those we see, the multitude we see not . . . whom misery, as well as sin, whom want of room, want of clothes, indol-ence, neglect or utter wretchedness, are shutting out from our fellowship . . . Yet there they surely are. In all our great towns thin walls separate luxury from starvation. The two classes live in absolute ignorance of each other . . . selfish respectability degrades one set; while misery and recklessness, which soon turns into vice and wickedness, weigh down the other.
(Samuel Wilberforce, *A Charge Delivered to the Clergy of the Archdeaconry of Surrey*, London, 1844, pp. 15–6)

Source 3.34 *The social classes in a country parish church (Barford, Warwickshire, in the 1830s)*
. . . In the parish church, the poor man and his wife were shown pretty plainly where they came among their fellow-creatures and fellow-worshippers . . . the poor were apportioned their lowly places and taught that they must sit in them Sunday after Sunday all their lives long. They must sit meekly and never dare to mingle with their betters in the social scale . . .

I can also remember the time when the parson's wife used to sit in state in her pew . . . and the poor women used to walk up the church and make a curtsey to her before taking the seats set apart for them. They were taught in this way that they had to pay homage and respect to those 'put in authority over them' . . .

. . . I saw what happened at that Communion service.

First, up walked the squire to the communion rails; the farmers went up next; then up went the tradesmen . . . and then, the very last of all, went the poor agricultural labourers in their smock frocks . . .

nobody else knelt with them; it was as if they were unclean . . .

(*Joseph Arch: the Story of his life*, Countess of Warwick ed., 1898, pp. 16–22)

Source 3.35 *A Chartist view of the teachings of the Church*

In the school and the church, the people are taught that passive obedience is a virtue . . . They are taught that they are mercifully created to endure poverty, and that the rich are very unfortunate in being born to the care and trouble of ruling over the poor. They are also taught, that God has created them poor, for the salvation of their immortal souls; and that through tribulation they must enter Heaven. They are taught that to fret at their earthly privations, is to rebel against the goodness of God, and for which they must incur his everlasting displeasure . . .

(*Chartist Circular*, 30 November 1839)

Source 3.36 *Industrial workers and the Church*

The people in agricultural districts are generally indifferent about the church . . . the upper and middle classes uphold her; but in the manufacturing districts she is the object of detestation to the working classes . . . The working classes consider themselves to be an oppressed people . . . they consider the Church to belong to the party of their oppressors; hence they hate it, and consider a man of the working classes who is a Churchman to be a traitor to his Party or Order – he is outlawed in the society in which he moves. Paupers and persons in need may go to church on the principle of living on the enemy; but woe to the young man in health and strength who proclaims himself a Churchman.

(From a letter sent by Dr Farquhar Hook, Vicar of Leeds to Archdeacon Samuel Wilberforce, 5 July 1843, in A. R. Ashwell, *Life of the Right Reverend Samuel Wilberforce*, London, 1880–2, vol. 1, p. 265)

Methodists and Evangelicals

Other churches were more active in social matters than the Church of England. The Methodist Church was founded by John Wesley in the eighteenth century. Methodists believed in carrying their Christian message to working people in the industrial towns and cities, often at mass meetings in the open air. They encouraged ordinary churchgoers to become involved in the organisation of their Methodist chapels.

Of course, not everyone in the Church of England was uncaring about the social problems of the time. Within the Church, there was the

Evangelical group. They shared the Methodists' concern for the poor, and were enthusiastic about social reforms to help working people. Some Evangelicals became famous for their good deeds. William Wilberforce worked for the abolition of the slave trade in 1807, and for the abolition of slavery in the British Empire in 1833. Lord Ashley, who became the Earl of Shaftesbury in 1851, devoted his life to improving conditions in factories and mines and helping neglected children.

Source 3.37 *Methodism in a country parish*

There was no chapel in our village, but when I was about fourteen years of age some dissenters (Methodists) began to come over from Wellsbourne. They used to hold meetings in a back lane. When the parson got wind of it, he and his supporters, the farmers, dared the labourers to go near these unorthodox Christians. If we did, then good-bye to all the charities; no more soup and coals should we have . . . I well remember going with my mother to listen to these dissenters. They used to preach under an old barn in the back lane. Rough and ready men were they . . . earnest and devoted to the truth as they saw it, good men all . . .

(*Joseph Arch: The Story of His Life*, Countess of Warwick ed., 1898, p. 22)

Source 3.38 *The Effects of the work of the Methodists*

The disciples of John Wesley gained a footing, and threw open the doors of Christ's kingdom to all. They moved among the poor; and by their earnestness and self-sacrifice, gained the love and reverence of the care-worn . . . The extent and nature of Wesleyan influence among the neglected classes were soon manifest, and not the least of the benefits it conferred, was the partial awakening of the members of other churches to a sense of their neglect in reference to their poor brethren . . .

(John Glyde, *The Moral, Social and Religious Condition of Ipswich*, 1850, S. R. Publishers, 1971 edition, p. 225)

Source 3.39 *Lord Ashley's choice of a career*

First, I must now choose my line of life . . . I see nothing but a political career . . . Where can I be so useful as in the public service? I am bound to try what God has put into me for the benefit of Old England! . . and having throughout desired nothing but this glory and the consummation [carrying-out] of His word, conclude in the same, to the advancement of religion and the increase of human happiness.

(Shaftesbury's Diary, 17 December 1827, in E. Hodder, *The Life and Work of . . . Shaftesbury*, London, 1887, pp. 43–4)

1. From source 3.33 which class of people regularly attended church in the early 1800s? Who were 'the multitude we see not'?

2. Is the working man's opinion of the church described in source 3.36 consistent with the evidence in sources 3.34 and 3.35? Do you think that most members of the government would have agreed with the teachings of the church in 3.35, or with the working man's view in 3.36?

3. From sources 3.37 and 3.38, say why the Methodists might appeal more to working men than the Church of England did.

4. Look at the Church's teachings as described in 3.35 and Lord Ashley's attitude in 3.39. What was the difference between the Church of England and the Evangelicals' attitude towards the poor?

Social Reform

Improving Public Health – the Work of Edwin Chadwick

As we saw in Chapter 2, Edwin Chadwick was among those responsible for the new Poor Law of 1834 and was one of the Poor Law Commissioners. In his work as a Poor Law Commissioner he became aware of the worsening living conditions in the towns, and led the campaign to improve public health and wipe out disease. To find out exactly what living conditions were like for working people, he appointed Doctors Kay, Arnott and Southwood-Smith to investigate housing conditions in East London. The registration of births, marriages and deaths had became compulsory in 1836, and these records helped their work greatly. The evidence produced by these men revealed for the first time to the middle class and the goverment the conditions in which most working people lived.

As a result, the government set up a Royal Commission in 1839, again headed by Chadwick, to carry out a nation-wide survey. Chadwick's 'Report on the Sanitary Conditions of the Labouring Population of Great Britain' in 1842 was the most detailed examination of the problem up to that time.

Chadwick's findings

Source 3.40   First, as to the extent and operation of the evils which are the subject of this enquiry –

That the various forms of epidemic, endemic and other diseases caused ... amongst the labouring classes by atmospheric impurities produced by decomposing animal and vegetable substances, by damp and filth, and close overcrowded dwellings prevail amongst the population in every part of the kingdom.

... that where these circumstances are removed by drainage, proper cleansing, better ventilation, and other means ... the frequency and intensity of such disease is abated ...

That the formation of all habits of cleanliness is obstructed by defective supplies of water.

(*Parliamentary Papers*, 1842, vol. 26, pp. 369–72)

Source 3.41 *Comparing the health of townspeople (Manchester) with country people (Rutland)*
You have seen the returns of the average ages of death amongst the different classes of people in Manchester and Rutland:

Average age of death	In Manchester	In Rutland (shire)
Professional persons and gentry and families	38	52
Tradesmen and their families	20	41
Mechanics, labourers and families	17	38

(Evidence presented in Chadwick's 'Report on the Sanitary Conditions of the Labouring Population of Great Britain', 1842)

Chadwick's recommendations

Chadwick pointed out that a national body would have to be set up to organise sanitary improvements, because huge engineering schemes would be required to improve drainage and sewerage throughout the country.

Source 3.42 The primary and most important measures, and at the same time the most practicable . . . are drainage, the removal of all refuse of habitations, streets, and roads, and the improvement of the supplies of water . . .
   That for the prevention of the disease occasioned by defective ventilation . . . where large numbers are assembled . . . that it would be a good economy to appoint a district medical officer independent of private practice, and with the . . . responsibility to initiate sanitary measures . . .

(Report from Poor Law Commissioners on an 'Enquiry into the Sanitary Condition of the Labouring Population of Great Britain', *Parliamentary Papers*, 1842, pp. 369–72)

Source 3.43 *Chadwick's reasons for public health reforms*
That the expense of public drainage, of supplies of water laid on in houses, and of means of improving cleansing would be a pecuniary gain [saving of money], by diminishing the existing charges attendant on sickness and premature mortality.

(*Parliamentary Papers*, 1842, vol. 26, pp. 369–72)

Source 3.44 *Chadwick's belief in the effect of his proposals*
That by the combinations of all these arrangements, it is probable that . . . an increase of 13 years at least, may be extended to the whole [life] of the labouring classes.

(*Parliamentary Papers*, 1842)

The 1848 Public Health Act

In spite of all Chadwick's shocking evidence about sanitary conditions in Britain, the government did little in the next few years to improve public health, except to appoint another Royal Commission in 1843. This meant that local authorities were left to find their own solutions to the problems which were affecting all large towns and cities. In 1848, Parliament at last passed the 1848 Public Health Act, but only because there was a very severe outbreak of cholera in that year. This was an important breakthrough in public health, even if it was not to last very long.

Source 3.45 *The Public Health Act, 1848*

1. A Central Board of Health was set up in London.
   (Chadwick and Lord Ashley were two of its original members.)
2. Local Boards of Health were set up in areas where either 10% of rate-payers asked for them, or where the death rate was higher than 23 per 1000 each year.
3. A Local Board could appoint a Medical Officer of Health, and it could raise rates for public health measures (such as installing sewers, providing a water-supply).
4. Local Boards could follow suggestions made by the Central Board, but were not forced to do so.

One important suggestion made by Chadwick at the Central Board was for the laying of narrow pipe-sewers. Sewage could be more easily flushed along this kind of sewer than along the large, brick-lined sewers which some cities used.

Source 3.46 A Meeting of the Central Board of Health in London, 1849

Source 3.47 *Sanitary improvements in Darlington*
Their [that is, diseases] coming was looked for, and all the appliances that science could devise were put . . . to meet the calamity. Water had been introduced into our streets . . . new sewers and drains . . . were in effective operation . . . cesspools abolished . . . and an efficient force of scavengers employed in removing all refuse from our streets . . . when epidemic diseases again appeared they could not maintain a footing in the old haunts where they formerly lingered . . . I may mention that the death-rate has fallen from 68 to 23 per 1000.

(*Annual Report*, 1855, of Dr Stephen Edward Piper, Medical Officer of Health for Darlington, 1851–82)

Source 3.48 Darlington Local Board of Health

DARLINGTON
LOCAL BOARD OF HEALTH.

The Board purpose at their next Meeting, to appoint the following Officers, viz:—

A COLLECTOR of Rates, a SURVEYOR, and an INSPECTOR of NUISANCES,

And will receive Written Proposals from Applicants.

The Collector will be required to find approved Security for **£300.**

The proposals for the Offices of Surveyor and Inspector of Nuisances, may be made to undertake them either together or separately.

Information as to the precise nature of the duties of each office may be obtained on *personal* application at my office, and sealed proposals stating the remuneration required, and indorsed " Application for the office of ———— to The Darlington Local Board of Health," (and in the case of the Collector with the names of the proposed Security) must be sent to me not later than Twelve o'clock at noon, on Thursday the 17th Instant.

The Board give no pledge to accept the lowest offers.

By order, **JOHN S. PEACOCK,**

CLERK TO THE BOARD.

Darlington, October 8th, 1850.

J. MANLEY, PRINTER, 41 HIGH ROW, DARLINGTON.

Source 3.49 *A less active Local Board of Health*
That in consequence of the Cholera having for some days ceased in this District, the Board consider they may dispense with the services of Dr Camps.

(Minutes of the Bridgend, Glamorgan, Board of Health, 20 November 1854)

Opposition to the Public Health Act

By 1854, local Boards of Health had been set up in nearly 300 areas, and they carried out improvements in public health which affected over two million people. In spite of this good work, there was considerable opposition to the Public Health Act and the Board of Health in London. Most governments at that time, and most people from the upper and middle classes believed in the idea of *laissez-faire*. They thought that the government should not interfere in people's everyday lives. They thought Chadwick in particular was an interfering busybody. Local authorities resented what they saw as interference in local affairs by the government.

The enemies of the Board of Health used their influence in Parliament and with the government to force Chadwick's resignation in 1853, and to cause the Board of Health to be abolished in 1854. Even so, Chadwick had proved to everyone beyond all doubt what living conditions were like for most of the people of Britain, and more public health measures were carried out by governments from the 1870s.

Source 3.50 *Against Public Health measures*
We prefer to take our chance with the cholera than be bullied into health. There is nothing a man hates so much as being cleansed against his will or having his floors swept, his halls whitewashed, his dung-heaps cleared away and his thatch forced to give way to slate. It is a fact that many people have died from a good washing. The truth is that Mr Chadwick has a great many powers but it is not so easy to say what they can be applied to. Perhaps a retirement pension with nothing to do will be a way of rewarding this gentleman.

(*The Times* quoted in Simon Masson, *Social Problems*, Blackwell, p. 17)

Source 3.51 *The Board of Health describing opposition to its work*
. . . We are aware that, in the discharge of [our] duties . . . we have unavoidably interfered with powerful interests, which have the immediate means of making themselves heard by members of Government and by Parliament . . .

. . . The scheme we proposed for extra-mural burial [not in the overcrowded cemeteries] endangered . . . cemetery companies and the entire body of trading undertakers.

. . . The report in condemnation of the present . . . supply of water to the Metropolis [London] necessarily excited the hostility of the existing water companies . . .

. . . the recommendation of the Commissioners for improving the Health of Towns, that surveys should be completed in detail before new works were undertaken . . . into the efficiency and economy of the plans for town drainage and water supply, caused the active hostility of professional engineers who were unaccustomed to such checks, and were now called upon . . . to reduce . . . their emoluments [profits].'

(Report of the Board of Health on its Work, *Parliamentary Papers*, 1848 XXXV, pp. 48–54)

_____ **Using the Evidence** _____

1. Look at sources 3.40 and 3.41.
    (a) What point was Chadwick making in comparing how long people lived in Rutland (a country area) and Manchester (a large industrial city)?
    (b) Which class had the shortest average life-span? From earlier evidence, would you expect this, or find it surprising? Give a reason for your answer.
    (c) Most people in governments in the early nineteenth century came from the upper class. How does source 3.41 help to explain why governments took so long to improve sewerage, water supply and housing standards for working people?

2. Look at sources 3.42 to 3.44.
    (a) What public health measures did Chadwick propose?
    (b) Find why Chadwick felt public health was so important. Write a sentence on each of the following, to explain Chadwick's reasons –
       (i) Helping the government
       (ii) Helping the people

3. Look at sources 3.45 to 3.49.
   (a) What public health improvements did the Darlington Local Board of Health carry out?
   (b) What were the different attitudes to public health improvements of the Darlington (sources 3.47 and 3.48) and Bridgend (source 3.49) Local Boards of Health? What weakness does this show in the working of the 1848 Public Health Act (3.45)?

4. From sources 3.50 and 3.51, make a list of those people who were against the working of the Boards of Health. Against each one, choose its reason from the following list:
   – would earn smaller fees
   – would not sell so much water
   – could not be bothered to live in a cleaner way
   – would lose money if overcrowded cemeteries were no longer used.
   How would you describe the attitude of these people, considering all the evidence Chadwick had produced about the causes of disease?

Improving Conditions in Factories and Mines

The 'Ten Hours Movement'

The fight for the 1833 Factory Act

Early factory acts in 1802 and 1819 had tried to improve working conditions for pauper children and for very young children. But factory owners usually ignored these laws because these was no way to enforce them.

In the early 1830s, the campaign to ensure a ten-hour maximum working day really got under way. It was begun by Richard Oastler, a Tory land agent, and was supported by well-meaning factory owners such as John Fielden and John Wood.

Source 3.52 The British factory worker and the West Indian slave

Source 3.53 *Oastler's letter to the* Leeds Mercury

Let truth speak out, appalling as the statement may appear. The fact is true. Thousands of our fellow creatures and fellow subjects, both male and female, the miserable inhabitants of a *Yorkshire town* . . . are at this very moment existing in a state of slavery, more *horrid* than are the victims of that hellish system *'colonial slavery'* . . . The very streets which receive the droppings of an 'Anti-Slavery Society' are every morning wet by the tears of innocent victims at the accursed shrine of avarice [greed], who are *compelled* (not by the cartwhip of the negro slave-driver) but by the dread of the equally appalling thong or strap of the over-looker, to hasten, half dressed, *but not half fed*, to those magazines of British infantile slavery – *the worsted mills in the town and neighbourhood of Bradford!*

(Richard Oastler, *Leeds Mercury*, 16 October 1830)

In Parliament, the campaign was led by Michael Sadler, a Tory MP and friend of Oastler. He introduced a bill to limit working hours for children to ten hours a day. Parliament would not pass the bill but it did set up a committee to find out more about factory conditions, with Sadler as chairman. When Sadler lost his seat in Parliament after the Parliamentary Reform Act of 1832, the Tory Lord Ashley took over leadership of the 'Ten Hours Movement' in Parliament.

Lord Ashley was one of the greatest philanthropists of the nineteenth century. That is, he devoted his life to improving conditions for working people, especially for children. As a Tory landowner, he held some traditional Tory views, such as opposing reform of Parliament. But he was a member of the Evangelical

Lord Ashley

movement in the Church of England, and his deep religious beliefs made him enthusiastic about helping those in need. In 1851, after the death of his father, he became the 7th Earl of Shaftesbury.

Ashley re-introduced Sadler's bill, but many MPs were still against intervening in factory conditions. They delayed by asking for still more information about factory conditions Another committee was set up, this time headed by Edwin Chadwick. Its findings persuaded Parliament to pass Althorp's Act, or the 1833 Factory Act, introduced by the Whig leader, Althorp.

Source 3.54 *The terms of the 1833 Factory Act (Althorp's Act)*

In all textile factories except silk mills –
1. Employment of children under 9 was banned.
2. Children from 9 to 13 were to work no more than 9 hours a day (48 hours a week), and had to have 2 hours schooling provided by the factory owner.
3. Young people between 13 and 18 were to work no more than 12 hours a day (69 hours a week).
4. Four factory inspectors were appointed to ensure factory owners obeyed the law.

Source 3.55 A Factory Inspector at work

FACTORIES REGULATION ACT, 7 Vic. c. 15.

No. *108*

CERTIFICATE of AGE for a CHILD to be Employed in the Factory of *Tho. Greg & Co*

Situated at Quarry Bank Styal in the County of Chester

I, *Joseph Nightingale of Wilmslow* duly appointed a Certifying Surgeon, do hereby certify That *Catherine Davenport*, Daughter

of *Sarah Davenport*

residing in *Pownallfee* has been personally examined by me, this *nineteenth*

day of *October* One thousand eight hundred and *fifty*; and that the said Child has the ordinary Strength and Appearance of a Child of at least EIGHT YEARS of Age, and that I believe the real Age of the said Child to be at least Eight Years; and that the said Child is not incapacitated, by Disease or bodily Infirmity, from working daily in the above-named Factory for the time allowed by this Act.

(Signed) *Joseph Nightingale* Certifying Surgeon.

Source 3.56 A Birth Certificate

Source 3.57 *Doubts about the working of the 1833 Factory Act*

We repeat, without watchfulness . . . the present law . . . will become a dead letter. For there are arrayed against it powerful interests . . . There is the interest of the master to whom the strict observance of the regulations . . . must still cause more trouble and expense. There is the interest of the advocate for imposing restriction on adult labour who, in order to demonstrate that there is no true remedy for the evils of the factory system but the Ten-hour Bill, will do anything in his power to counteract the working of [the] measure.

(From the *London and Westminster Review*, October 1836)

The continuing struggle

Factory reformers regarded the 1833 Act as only the beginning of the campaign that would lead to a ten-hour working day for all. In factory areas, Short Time Committees were formed to continue the struggle. Their members were working men, but also some factory owners who were friendly to their cause, like John Fielden. These committees worked closely with the leaders of the factory movement in Parliament, like Lord Ashley (see source 3.58). Pressure from inside and outside Parliament resulted in the Factory Act of 1844 and the 'Ten Hours Act' of 1847 (see 3.59 and 3.60).

Source 3.58 A leaflet advertising a meeting of Short Time Committees in Manchester

THE TEN HOURS' BILL.

TO THE FACTORY OPERATIVES OF LANCASHIRE.

FELLOW WORKPEOPLE,

The present position of the Ten Hours' Bill now before the House of Commons demands your most serious attention. On your exertions, in a very great degree, depends the success or failure of our present struggle. The Central Committee, ever anxious to consult the factory workers in such times of difficulty, have deemed it their duty to call a Delegate Meeting from every town in Lancashire, to consider the best course now to be adopted, and to lay down certain rules to guide the delegates in their course of procedure in London. A statement of the accounts of the Committee will be laid before the meeting, and every other information which they possess.

The meeting will be held on Sunday, April 19th, 1846, at the OLD SWAN INN, *Pool Street, Market Street*, near the Post Office, Manchester.

It is particularly requested that each district will send at least one delegate, as the business to be brought before the meeting will be important.

Before the time of meeting Lord Ashley and Mr. Fielden will be communicated with on the subject, and their advice taken as to what is the best course to be adopted, which will, of course, be laid before the meeting.

The Chair to be taken at Ten o'clock in the Morning precisely.

JOSEPH MULLINEAUX, SEC.

N.B.—All communications in future to be addressed to the Secretary, Old Swan Inn, Pool Street, Market Street, Manchester.

Source 3.59 *The 1844 Factory Act*

1. Women's hours were limited to 12 a day.
2. The minimum age at which a child could work in a factory was lowered from 9 to 8 years.
3. Children from 8 to 13 had their hours of work reduced from 9 to 6½ a day.

Source 3.60 *The 'Ten Hours Act', 1847*

Working hours for women and 13–18 year olds were limited to 10 a day.

Now that women and children could work no more than ten hours a day, Ashley thought that men too would be restricted to a ten-hour day (see source 3.61). But many factory owners avoided this by a 'relay' system of women and children working different shifts, so that factories could be kept open for more than ten hours a day. Parliament was still reluctant to pass laws affecting the working hours of men (see source 3.62) but Ashley kept up the struggle and accepted a compromise without consulting the representatives of factory workers. The result was the 1850 Factory Act (see 3.63). It so disappointed working men in the 'Ten Hours Movement' that they would no longer accept Ashley's leadership.

Source 3.61 *Ashley's reaction to the 'Ten Hours Act'*
We have now won the object of all our labours – the Ten Hours Bill has become the law of the land; and we may hope, nay, we believe, that we shall find in its happy results, a full compensation for all our toils . . .

(Lord Ashley's letter to the Short Time Committees; in E. Hodder, *The Life and Work of the Seventh Earl of Shaftesbury*, 1892, p. 369)

Source 3.62 *Against passing laws on men's working conditions*
Even the best institutions can give a man no active aid. Perhaps the utmost they can do is, to leave him *free* to develop himself and improve his individual condition . . . there is no power of law that can make the idle man industrious, the thriftless provident, or the drunken sober; . . .'

(Samuel Smiles, *Self-help*, 1859, pp. 1–2)

Source 3.63 *The 1850 Factory Act*

A 10½-hour maximum working day was introduced for all workers over 13 years of age.

The Mines Act of 1842

Ashley also persuaded Parliament to set up a Commission to investigate working conditions in the mines. The public was shocked by the evidence of the Mines Commission (see source 3.64 below). Parliament was convinced of the need to intervene, despite the opposition of many powerful mine owners, such as Lord Londonderry (see source 3.65 below). Ashley introduced a Bill which eventually became the Mines Act of 1842. No women or girls were to be employed underground, nor boys under ten years old. Inspectors were appointed to make sure mine owners kept to the law, and to make recommendations for safety improvements.

Source 3.64 *Public reaction to the evidence of the Mines Commission*
Here . . . we have disclosed to use – in our own land . . . modes [ways] of existence . . . which are as strange and as new as the wildest dreams of fiction . . .

Here we find tens of thousands of our countrymen living apart from the rest of the world . . .

It is mainly to Lord Ashley, who has headed this great movement for the moral improvement of the working classes, that we are indebted for these volumes, issued apparently for the purpose of letting the public know the true condition of the mining population . . . the whole state of the mines as to care, ventilation, draining, and as to employment of women, reads so miserably, that we . . . would hope the account overdrawn.

. . . Is the contractor alone at fault? . . . Or shall we blame the parents and relations, by whose avarice [greed] . . . these females are thus subjected to . . . evils of the worst kind? On both sides the guilt is great – very great – but surely vastly greater in him who has not even the excuse of poverty for receiving 'the thirty pieces of silver' . . .

(*Quarterly Review*, lxx, 1842 p. 158 seq.)

Source 3.65 *Lord Londonderry against the 'Report of the Mines Commission'*
[Lord Londonderry] said that it appeared that the Commissioners had come to this inquiry fresh from the Factory Commission . . . and with an expectation and desire of finding similar oppressions amongst the miners to those which they had found amongst the manufacturing population . . . and the mode [way] in which they collected their evidence – communicating with artful boys and ignorant young girls, and putting questions in a manner which in many cases seemed to suggest the answer, was anything but . . . fair and impartial . . . he thought the Report had been accompanied by pictures of [a] disgusting and . . .

scandalous ... character was not such as should have been adopted in a grave publication ...

... (His Lordship [said] the following:) The trapper's employment is neither cheerless, dull nor stupefying ... The trapper is generally cheerful and contented, and to be found, like other children of his age, occupied with some childish amusement – as cutting sticks, making models of windmills, waggons etc. ...

(*Hansard*, House of Lords, 24 June 1842)

Source 3.66 A family meeting father from the pit

Using the Evidence

1. Look at sources 3.52 and 3.53
   (a) Who is the speaker in the centre of 3.52 saying was better off – the West Indian slave or the factory worker in Britain?
   (b) Which of these two seems to be better off and which worse off, in the picture?
   (c) Which did Richard Oastler say was worse off, in source 3.53?
   (d) What is the point the cartoonist is trying to make?

2. Construct a table like the one below to summarise the details about the different Factory Acts.

Act	Supporters	Terms	Good points	Faults
1833	Sadler Oastler Ashley			

3. How would a factory inspector like the one in source 3.55 be helped by the compulsory registration of births in 1836? (see source 3.56).

4. Which illustration do you think presents the truer picture of factory children – source 3.55 (Factory Inspector at work) or source 3.18 on p. 61 (The Mill Children)?

5. Why did working men and women in the Short Time Committees think it was so important to have people like Lord Ashley and John Fielden on their side in the 'Ten Hours Movement'?

6. 'We have now won the object of all our labours' (Ashley – source 3.61). How was Ashley wrong about the effect of the 1847 'Ten Hours Act'?

7. Look at source 3.64. Why was the writer in the *Quarterly Review* so shocked at conditions in the mines? (Look back to the section Working in the Mines pp. 63–5.)

8. Does Lord Londonderry's description of the life of a trapper (source 3.65) agree with the mine inspector's report in source 3.29 on p. 65? Why do you think he said the trapper was so contented in his work? Why did he say that the 1842 'Report on Conditions in the Mines' was (in his opinion) not an accurate one?

Coursework

Continuity and Change

Compare a factory boy's or girl's working life before 1833 (see pp. 59–61) with his or her life in 1851. How would the child's life have been improved, and what improvements in working conditions had still not been made by 1851?

78

Elizabeth Fry and Prison Reform

Local bodies were responsible at this time for the organisation of prisons. As a result there were many types of prison – county gaols, town gaols and even private gaols belonging to some nobles and bishops. Many local magistrates avoided their duty of inspecting prisons, so that in most prisons, conditions were very bad. Gaolers were unpaid, and 'earned' their income by charging fees from the prisoners. With the great increase of crime in the industrial areas, the number of prisoners increased, and prison conditions worsened still further.

Mrs Elizabeth Fry was a Quaker, a member of the church called The Society of Friends. Her religious beliefs made her try to improve prison conditions. Her visits to Newgate prison in London – one of the worst prisons in Britain – shocked her into forming the Association for the Improvement of Women Prisoners in Newgate.

Source 3.67 *Elizabeth Fry's first visit to Newgate, 1817*
She found the female side in a situation which no language can describe. Nearly *three hundred women*, sent there for every gradation of crime, some untried, and some under sentence of death, were crowded together in two wards and two cells ... Here they saw their friends, and kept their multitudes of children; and they had no other place for cooking, washing, eating and sleeping.

They all slept on the floor; ... without so much as a mat for bedding; ... She saw them openly drinking spirits; and her ears were offended by the most dreadful imprecations [oaths]. Everything was filthy to excess, and the smell was quite disgusting. Every one, even the Governor, was reluctant to go amongst them.

(Thomas Fowell Buxton, *An Enquiry Whether Crime and Misery are Produced or Prevented by our present System of Prison Discipline*, London, 1818)

Mrs Fry believed that being imprisoned was not for revenge on the criminal, but to improve his or her behaviour and prevent further crime. She tried to get prisoners to behave better and made suggestions for improvements in running the prison. She strongly believed that religious instruction and reading the Bible would greatly improve the behaviour of criminals.

Source 3.68 *Elizabeth Fry's work at Newgate*
The next day she commenced the school ... She felt as if she was going into a den of wild beasts; and she well recollects quite shuddering when the door closed upon her, and she was locked in, with such a herd of ... desperate companions. This day, however, the school surpassed their utmost expectations; their only pain arose from the numerous and pressing applications made by young women, who longed to be taught and employed ... they tempted these ladies to project a school for the employment of the tried women, for teaching them to read and to work.

... they trusted it would receive the guidance and protection of Him, who often is pleased to accomplish the highest purposes by the most feeble instruments.

With these impressions, they had the boldness to declare, that if a committee could be found who would share the labour, and a matron who would engage never to leave the place ... they would undertake to try the experiment ...

(Thomas Fowell Buxton, *An Enquiry Whether Crime and Misery are Produced or Prevented by our Present System of Prison Discipline*, London, 1818)

Source 3.69 *Elizabeth Fry's ideal prison*
I should prefer a prison where women were allowed to work together in companies with proper super intendance, and their recreation also; to have their meals together, under proper superintendance ... Their being in company during the day tends, under proper regulation, to the advancement of principle and industry, for it affords a stimulus. I would think solitary confinement proper in only very atrocious cases.

(John Kent, *Elizabeth Fry*, p. 80)

Source 3.70 *Mrs Fry's prison rules*
2. That the women be engaged in needlework, knitting or any other suitable employment.
3. That there be no begging, swearing, gaming, card-playing, quarrelling, or immoral conversation ...
10. That at the ringing of the bell, at nine o'clock in the morning, the women collect in the work-room to hear a portion of scripture read by one of the visitors, or the matron ...

(*Memoir of Elizabeth Fry*, vol. 1, pp. 269–70)

Source 3.71 *The effect of scripture reading*
(1) After the reading is over, the company sits for a few minutes in perfect silence ... the word of Scripture ... appears to excite in prisoners much tenderness of mind; and we have sometimes observed during these periods of serious thought that almost every eye in the room has been wet with tears.

(Joseph Gurney, *Prisons in Scotland and the North of England*, p. 157)

(2) My readings at Newgate . . . are to my feelings too much like making a show of a good thing.

(Elizabeth Fry after a visit to Newgate in 1818. From *Memoir of Elizabeth Fry*, vol. 1, p. 345)

Source 3.72 *The effects of Elizabeth Fry's work at Newgate*

Many of these [visitors to Newgate] knew Newgate . . . and had not forgotten the painful impressions made by a scene exhibiting . . . the very utmost limits, of misery and guilt. They now saw, what, without exaggeration may be called a transformation. Riot . . . and filth, exchanged for order, sobriety, and comparative neatness in the chamber . . . They saw no more an assemblage of abandoned and shameless creatures . . . The prison no more resounded with obscenity . . . 'this hell on earth' already exhibited the appearance of an industrious manufactory, or a well-regulated family.

(Thomas Fowell Buxton, *An Enquiry Whether Crime and Misery are Produced or Prevented by our Present System of Prison Discipline*, London, 1818)

With her brother, Joseph Gurney, Elizabeth Fry visited prisons in the north of England and in Scotland to form prison associations like the one in Newgate. The rest of her life was dedicated to the cause of prison reform and, because of her efforts, the Home Secretary, Robert Peel, took action on prison conditions. His Prison Act of 1823 was the first step in improving prison conditions in the nineteenth century.

Source 3.74 *The Prison Act, 1823*

1. Prison buildings were to be roomy and sanitary.
2. Prisoners were to be separated, with hardened criminals kept apart from other offenders.
3. Jailers were to be paid, and they were prevented from receiving payment from prisoners.
4. Female warders were to supervise female prisoners.
5. Prisoners were to be given instruction in reading, writing and religion.
6. Chaplains and doctors were to visit prisons regularly.
7. Before chains or irons could be used on a prisoner, a Justice of the Peace had to give permission.

Source 3.73 Elizabeth Fry at Newgate

It was still up to local magistrates to enforce the Act, so it was still ignored in some areas, especially in many smaller prisons. But if magistrates did want to improve prison conditions, they now had Peel's Prison Act to help them. It was not until 1835 that the Home Secretary became responsible for prisons, and could appoint prison inspectors to enforce the law.

Using the Evidence

1. Look at source 3.67.
   (a) Make a list of all that was wrong with prison conditions at Newgate before Elizabeth Fry's visit.
   (b) Why must it have taken a lot of courage for Mrs Fry to have gone to Newgate prison?

2. How might Mrs Fry have been surprised at the reaction of women prisoners to her? (See source 3.68.)

3. From what you have found out about Elizabeth Fry (including from sources 3.68 and 3.69) suggest what Mrs Fry's reasons were for her prison rules in source 3.70. Construct a table like this for your answers:

Mrs Fry's Rules	Her reasons for the rules
That the women be engaged in needlework, etc.	

4. Look at source 3.71 (1) and (2). Is there any reason to doubt that religious instruction had a good effect on prisoners?

5. Use sources 3.67 and 3.72 to compare Newgate prison before and after Mrs Fry's work there. Again, put your answers in a table. (An example has been given to start you off.)

Before	After
The prison was filthy	It had been made comparatively tidy

Coursework

Continuity and Change

1. Look at the beginning of this section to find out about prison conditions before the 1820s. Would Peel's Prison Act of 1823 have put right everything that was wrong with prisons, even if it could have been properly enforced?

2. Make a list of prison improvements you feel should have been carried out in addition to Peel's measures.

The Education of the People

Today, most children attend a state school, that is, a school provided with government help, which is part of a national system of education. The situation was completely different in the early nineteenth century. At that time, governments did not think it was their job to provide education for everyone. In fact, many Members of Parliament were against any proper education for working-class children (Source 3.75).

The rich could afford to pay for their children's education. Sons of the rich went to fee-paying Public schools such as Eton, Harrow, Winchester and Rugby. There, they learned Latin and Greek and were strictly disciplined. Upper-class girls were usually educated at home by governesses, who taught them reading, writing, poetry and music. Middle-class parents who could not afford Public-school fees often sent their children to Grammar schools and Academies, where the fees were lower. Grammar schools taught mainly Latin and Greek, but Academies had a wider range of subjects – English, classics, science, book-keeping and navigation.

Although the standard of education in Public schools, Grammar schools and Academies was usually poor, at least children from better-off families had the opportunity to learn. Children from poorer homes received only a little education, or none at all (Source 3.76).

Source 3.75 *A Member of Parliament against educating the people*
... giving education to the labouring classes of the poor, would, in effect, ... lead them to despise their lot in life, instead of making them good servants in agriculture and other laborious employments to which their rank in society had destined them; ... it would enable them to read seditious pamphlets [pamphlets which opposed the government], vicious books and publications against Christianity; it would render them insolent to their superiors. Besides, it would burden the country with an enormous expense.
(David Giddy MP in a Parliamentary debate, July 1807)

Source 3.76 *A Yorkshireman remembers his education in the 1820s*
There were very few schools, and many of the teachers could not have passed our present Board Schools' sixth standard [Primary Six]. Some taught nothing but reading and spelling, or knitting and sewing; others only reading and writing from printed copies ... A few taught arithmetic as well, but a grammar, geography, or history were scarcely ever seen in a school in those days ... Large numbers never entered the door of a schoolhouse – having to work at something when they arrived at school age, or were allowed to run about all day, as if they were mere animals ... writing was looked upon by many parents as a mere luxury for the rich only, and never likely to be wanted by their sons and daughters. A person who was a good reader of the newspaper, and could talk about various wars, battles, and sieges, was looked up to by the people, and said to be a 'great scholar' and a 'far-learned man'.
(Joseph Lawson, *Progress in Pudsey*, Stanningley 1887, pp. 39–42)

Different kinds of schools

In Scotland, some attempt had been made to provide education for all. By law, there had to be a school in each parish, with a teacher and school-room paid for by local landowners. Though standards varied, this provided a better education than was available for most children in England. There, some children went to Charity schools. These were first set up by the Society for the Propagation of Christian Knowledge in 1699. Using money left to them by well-meaning people, they taught both boys and girls religion, reading, writing and arithmetic, and practical skills such as weaving, gardening and knitting. But only children whose parents were members of the Church of England were allowed to attend Charity schools, and their names had to be put forward by the people who left money to the schools. So most children could not attend Charity schools.

Sunday schools were the first to try to provide an education for many working-class children. The first was set up in 1783 by Robert Raikes, a newspaper owner from Gloucester, after seeing factory children playing on a Sunday. Source 3.77 is part of a letter written by Raikes replying to an enquiry about Sunday schools.

Source 3.77 SIR   *Gloucester, Nov 25*
Some business leading me one morning into the suburbs of the city, where the lowest of the people ... chiefly reside, I was struck with concern at seeing a group of children, wretchedly ragged, at play in the street ... Ah! Sir, said the woman to whom I was speaking ... you would be shocked indeed; for then [Sunday] the street is filled with multitudes of these wretches, who, released on that day from employment, spend their time in noise and riot, playing at chuck, and cursing and swearing ... I then enquired of the woman, if there were any decent, well-disposed women in the neighbourhood, who kept

schools for teaching to read. I presently was directed to four . . . and made an agreement with them to receive as many children as I should send upon the Sunday, whom they were to instruct in reading, and in the church catechism . . .

(The *Gentlemen's Magazine*, 1783)

The first Ragged school was set up by a Portsmouth shoemaker, John Pounds in 1820, in his own tiny workshop, to teach poor children and orphans. Other caring people took up the idea and it soon spread to other parts of the country. Lord Ashley united the Ragged schools into the Ragged Schools Union in 1844 to spread the idea still further.

Source 3.78 The Lambeth Ragged School (*Illustrated London News*)

But Charity schools, Sunday schools and Ragged schools could only provide a very limited kind of education for a small number of children. Most working-class children in the growing industrial towns had no education at all. The first attempt to provide a cheap form of education for many more children was in Monitorial schools.

Monitorial schools were the idea of Joseph Lancaster, a Quaker, and Andrew Bell, a Church of England vicar. Their idea was that one teacher could look after hundreds of children, with the help of monitors, that is older children who were a step ahead of younger pupils. The teacher first taught a lesson to monitors who, in turn, taught it to the younger children.

Source 3.79 *Joseph Lancaster's description of his school*

My school is attended by near three hundred scholars. The whole system of tuition is almost entirely conducted by boys; . . . In the first instance, the school is divided into classes; to each of these a lad is appointed as monitor; he is responsible for the morals, improvement, good order and cleanliness of the whole class. It is his duty to make a daily, weekly and monthly report of progress, specifying the number of lessons performed, boys present, absent etc.

A monitor delivers out the leather commendatory tickets [awarded for good work], a second the tickets of the order of merit, another has a general charge as to cleanliness etc. and a fourth has the care of near three hundred slates. Thus every duty has its respective officer . . .

(Joseph Lancaster, *Improvements in Education as it Respects the Industrious classes*, 1803, pp. 45–6)

But Bell and Lancaster disagreed about the kind of religion to be taught in schools. Lancaster and his supporters were Nonconformists or Dissenters. They did not agree with the teachings of the Church of England. They set up the British and Foreign Schools Society for children of all religions. In 1811, Bell set up the National Society for children in the Church of England. Both groups provided primary education in monitorial schools supported by donations of money from the public. By 1830, there were 400 National Schools and 100 British and Foreign Schools.

Source 3.80 A Lancastrian School in Clapham, which used the monitorial system

Source 3.81 Pupil's Certificate from a National School

Source 3.82 Who shall educate? Or, Our Babes in the Wood (*Punch* 1853)

Robert Owen's school at New Lanark

We have already seen on p. 62 how Robert Owen, the part-owner and manager of the New Lanark Mills on the Clyde cared for the needs of his workers, unlike most factory owners of the time. As part of his plan for New Lanark village, Owen provided a school-room and nursery facilities for the New Lanark children.

Source 3.83 *Robert Owen's description of education at New Lanark*

. . . many of you, mothers of families, will be enabled to earn a better . . . support for your children . . . while the children will be prevented from acquiring any bad habits, and gradually prepared to learn the best.

. . . as they advance in years, they will be regularly instructed in the rudiments [basics] of common learning; which, before they shall be six years old, they may be taught in a superior manner . . . . they will be admitted into this place which is to be the general school-room for reading, writing, arithmetic, sewing and knitting; all which . . . will be accomplished . . by the time the children are ten years old . . . For the benefit of the health and spirits of the children, both boys and girls will be taught to dance . . . those of each sex who may have good voices will be taught to sing, and those among the boys who have a taste for music will be taught to play upon some instrument; for it is intended to give them as much diversified [varied] innocent amusement as . . . the establishment will permit.

In summer it is intended that they shall derive knowledge from a personal examination of the works of nature and of art, by going out frequently with some of their masters into the neighbourhood and country around.

(Robert Owen, *An address delivered to the inhabitants of New Lanark, on the first of January, 1816* . . . 2nd edn, London 1816)

Source 3.84 The school-room at New Lanark

The government and education

The government first took an interest in education because the Factory Act of 1833 said that working children between nine and twelve years should have at least two hours schooling a day (see page 74), and the 1844 Factory Act increased it to three hours a day. So it gave £20 000 a year divided between the National and Lancasterian (or British and Foreign) schools. In 1834, this sum was increased to £30 000, and even more money was given to the two school societies in the 1840s.

But the government was concerned about poor school buildings, unqualified teachers and many children not attending school regularly. It did not want its money to be wasted. So it decided to set up a Committee on Education in 1839. In this letter, Lord John Russell, a government minister, explained to Lord Lansdowne what the government intended to do.

Source 3.85 ... Among the chief defects yet existing may be reckoned the insufficient number of qualified school-masters, the imperfect mode [method] of teaching in ... the schools ...

... I am directed by Her Majesty to desire ... that your Lordship, with four others ... should form a board or Committee, for the consideration of all matters affecting the education of the people. ...

Among the first objects to which any grant may be applied will be the establishment of a Normal School.

In such a school a body of schoolmasters may be formed, competent to assume the management of similar institutions in all parts of the country. In such a school ... the best modes [methods] of teaching may be introduced, and those who wish to improve the schools of their neighbourhood may have an opportunity of observing their results.

(*Parliamentary Papers*, 1839, xII, pp. 255–7)

The Board did a great amount of good work, thanks to its able and enthusiastic Secretary, Dr James Kay-Shuttleworth. He had worked among the poor people of Manchester, and believed that the only way to improve conditions for working people was through proper education. Government inspectors were appointed to check on teaching standards in schools and to see that government money was being properly used. The first teacher-training college was set up at Battersea in 1840, and the government increased its grant to education to £100 000 a year in 1846. By this time, the pupil-teacher system was replacing the monitorial system. In the pupil-teacher system, a teacher could train his best

pupils from the age of 13 for five years. Then, they would be ready to become teachers themselves and start their own schools, if they wished.

Source 3.86 The Educational question (*Punch* 1853)

How much progress had there been in education?

To answer this question, the government set up the Newcastle Commission – a Royal Commission under the Duke of Newcastle. It reported in 1861 and had many criticisms of the state of education. It said most teachers were not able to teach properly, and that many children still did not attend regularly. Bad attendance was sometimes because parents could not even afford small fees, and often because of poor health. Many people doubted if it was possible to educate all children.

Source 3.87 *Evidence of the Rev. James Fraser to the Newcastle Commission*
I doubt whether it would be desirable, with a view to the real interests of the peasant boy, to keep him at school till he was 14 or 15 years of age. But it is not possible. We must make up our minds to see the last of him ... at 10 or 11 ... It is quite possible to teach a child ... all that is necessary for him to possess ... by the time that he is 10 years old ... He shall be able to spell correctly the words that he will ordinarily have to use; he shall read ... the paragraph in the newspaper that he cares to read – with sufficient ease to be a pleasure to himself and to convey information to listeners ... he knows enough of ciphering [counting] to make out ... a common shop bill; if he hears talk of foreign countries he has some notions

as to the part of the . . . globe in which they lie . . . he has acquaintance enough with the Holy Scriptures to follow . . . the arguments of a . . . sermon, and . . . to know what are the duties required of him . . .

I have no bright view of the future or the possibilities of an English elementary education floating before my eyes . . . what I have seen in the last six months would have . . . for ever dissipated them.

By 1850, about half of the people in Britain still could not read and write. It took until 1870 for the government to realise it had to do much more if everyone was to be properly educated. In that year (1872 in Scotland) the government passed an Education Act which said there should be locally elected School Boards to provide compulsory, free primary education for all. This was the real beginning of a state system of education.

Using the Evidence

1. Why did many MPs (like David Giddy in source 3.75) not want the government to provide education for the children of poorer families? Find *two* reasons and say which reason was the more important for David Giddy, in your view.

2. From source 3.76, find as many pieces of evidence as you can to show how poor the standard of education was for working-class children in Pudsey, Yorkshire. Look at the sentence beginning 'A person who was a good reader. . . .'. What does it tell you about most people's education at the time?

3. Look at source 3.77.
   (a) What was Robert Raikes reason for starting Sunday schools?
   (b) Why could the children not attend school on other days?

4. How would a teacher in a Monitorial school describe how he organised his school? (source 3.79) From source 3.80 identify the schoolmaster, the monitors and the pupils. Suggest a reason why pupils might not have been very well taught in this kind of school.

5. In source 3.82, what effect does the cartoonist suggest the argument between Lancaster (Dissent) and Bell (High Church) are having on the education of children?

6. What do the pictures and map on the walls in source 3.84 tell you about the education provided at New Lanark?

7. Look back to the education provided by Charity schools, Sunday schools and Monitorial schools. In what ways was the education at New Lanark better than in these schools? (See source 3.83.)

8. Owen was not just interested in the children being taught different subjects. How else would his school help the welfare of the children at New Lanark?

9. What criticisms does Lord John Russell make of education in source 3.85? What suggestions does he make for improving education?

10. What comment on the state of education is the cartoonist making in source 3.86?

11. Look at sources 3.75, 3.76 and 3.87.
    (a) Compare the Rev. James Fraser's attitude to educating the people in source 3.87 with that of David Giddy in source 3.75. How much difference do you think there is between the two men's views?
    (b) How much better an education would a child get if the Rev. James Fraser's views were followed, compared to the education there was in the 1820s described in 3.76?

Causation and Motivation

1. What kinds of school were there in the early nineteenth century for poor children to attend?

2. From these facts say why most poor children did not go to any of these schools, or only went occasionally:
   – children worked in factories from an early age
   – no one checked on a pupil's attendance
   – schooling was not free – at least a small fee had to be paid
   – in the past, poorer children had not gone to school.

3. Here are three reasons why the government began to take an interest in education from the 1830s onwards:
   (a) The passing of the 1833 and the 1844 Factory Acts
   (b) The government grants of money to education from 1833
   (c) Most children still received no education in spite of all the different kinds of schools
   Say why (a) and (b) made the government more interested in education. Which of (a), (b), and (c) do you think was a less important reason for the government's interest?

Continuity and Change

4. Do you think the standard of education for most of the people had improved much between 1815 and 1851? Give reasons for your answer.

4 Emigration

The Last Look at England
(Ford Madox Brown)

The period 1815 to 1851 was certainly one of great change. We have studied the nature of some of these changes in earlier chapters – the growth of factories, new ways of dealing with poverty, the extension of the franchise and so on. Behind all these developments lay an even more basic one – changes in population.

Source 4.1 *Population of Great Britain (excluding Ireland)*

1750	7.75 million
1801	10.69 "
1811	12.15 "
1821	14.21 "
1831	16.37 "
1841	18.55 "
1851	20.88 "

Source 4.2 *Population of Towns (thousands)*

	1801	1851
Birmingham	71	233
Bradford	13	104
Glasgow	77	329
Leeds	53	170
Liverpool	82	376
Manchester	70	303

Source 4.3 *The Census of 1851*

The most important result which the inquiry establishes, is the addition in half a century, of ten millions of people to the British population. The increase of population in the half of this century nearly equals the increase in all preceding ages . . .

Two other movements of the population have been going on in the United Kingdom: the immigration of the population of Ireland into Great Britain, and the constant flow of the country population into the towns . . . where the towns engage in a manufacture as one vast undertaking, in which nearly the whole population is concerned . . .

At the same time, too, that the population of the towns and of the countryside, have become so equally balanced in number – ten millions against ten millions . . .

(*Census of Great Britain, 1851*, vol. i, 1852 Report
Section 8, lxxxiii–lxxxiv)

Source 4.4 *Thomas Malthus's views on the population changes*

This ratio of increase . . . we will take it as our rule; and say,

That population, when unchecked, goes on doubling itself every twenty-five years, or increases in a geometrical ratio.

Let us now take any spot of earth, this island for instance, and see in what ratio the subsistence it affords can be supposed to increase. We will begin with it under its present state of cultivation.

If I allow that by the best present policy, the produce of this island may be doubled in the first twenty-five years, I think it will be allowing as much as any person can well demand.

In the next twenty-five years, it is impossible to suppose that the produce could be doubled. It would be contrary to [against] all our knowledge of the qualities of land. The very utmost that we can conceive, is, that the increase in the second twenty-five years might equal the present produce. Let us then take this for our rule, though certainly far beyond the truth; and allow that by great exertion, the whole produce of the island might be increased every twenty-five years, by a quantity of subsistence equal to what it at present produces.

Yet this ratio of increase is evidently arithmetical.

It may be fairly said, therefore, that the means of subsistence increase in an arithmetical ratio.

(Thomas R. Malthus, *An Essay on Population*, 1798,
pp. 21–3)

Reasons for Emigration

Population was thus increasing rapidly, and at the same time, industrial towns were growing almost overnight. Changes were also taking place in the countryside. Enclosures had meant that many poor people lost their right to land. New methods such as improved machinery left many domestic workers and agricultural labourers unemployed, and dependent on poor relief. To some of the middle and upper classes, this was further evidence of 'redundant' and excess population. Increasingly emigration came to be seen as a solution to the problems of over population and unemployment.

Source 4.5 Numbers of the miserables of this country were now migrating: they wandered in a state of desperation; too poor to pay, they madly sell themselves, for their passage, preferring a temporary bondage in a strange land, to starving for life on their native soil.

(Thomas Pennant, *A Tour in Scotland and Voyage to
the Hebrides 1772*, 1790, I, p. 405)

Source 4.6 An attentive and general observation of the present state of the Highlands and Islands, it is imagined, will fully warrant the assertion, that the great and most universally operating cause of emigration is that, in comparison of the means of subsistence they afford, these countries are greatly overstocked with persons.

(*Scots Magazine* vol. 54 pp. 56–7)

Source 4.7 They [the landless tenants] know that in ... the manufacturing towns, labour will procure them good wages; they know likewise that in America the wages of labour are still higher, and that from the moderate price of land they may expect to obtain not only the possession of a farm, but an absolute property.

(5th Earl of Selkirk, *Observations of the present state of the Highlands of Scotland*, 1805, p. 47)

Source 4.8 Copies of letters from persons who had emigrated several years before to America ... were circulated ...

(*Statistical Account of Scotland*, 1798, XIII, p. 317)

Source 4.9 *Emigrating Workman:*
'Goodbye, Mother! Sorry to leave you, but if you can't find me work, what can I do?'

Source 4.10 Here and There; or Emigration a Remedy, (*Punch*, 1848)

Source 4.11 First Letter from the Emigrants

_____ **Using the Evidence** _____

1. Look at sources 4.1, 4.2, 4.3.
   (a) Using source 4.1, draw a graph to show the change in population between 1750 and 1851.
   (b) Study source 4.2. Which town's population has grown at the fastest rate?
   (c) What explanation is given in 4.3 for the growth of the towns?

2. Study 4.4 carefully.
   (a) If Malthus was correct, what should the population total have been by 1851, assuming that it was ten million in 1801?
   (b) Look at 4.2 and 4.3 again. Why do you think Malthus thought the population was growing so rapidly?
   (c) Malthus's *Essay* was widely read after it was published in 1798. What effect do you think it might have had on people?

3. Sources 4.5 to 4.7, 4.9, 4.10 give some of the reasons for people deciding to emigrate.
   (a) Briefly list the reasons given.
   (b) Some of these reasons are '*push*' reasons, saying why people left Britain; others are '*pull*' reasons, saying why people were attracted to lands abroad. Which of the reasons you have listed are 'push' or 'pull' ones? Which of the sources provides both?

4. Look at sources 4.8 and 4.11.
   (a) How does the artist of 4.11 show that the people there are greatly interested in how the emigrants are doing?
   (b) What effect is the writer of 4.8 perhaps suggesting that these letter-reading sessions might have?

Attitudes to Emigration

At first government and landowners were generally opposed to emigration, fearing that there would be less men available for the army. After the war with France ended in 1815, attitudes began to change. Agricultural depression had set in, leading to rising poor rates and bankruptcies for farmers and unemployment and discontent for workers. Emigration offered a possible solution.

Source 4.12 *An MP's View*

... there existed a redundancy of able-bodied and active labourers, with their families, for whose labours there was no effective demand in either Ireland, Scotland, or England. The effect of this redundancy was, to reduce the wages of the labourer much below the proper level: and the consequence was, destitution and misery amongst great masses of the poor ... He should also mention, that the committee never in any way recommended any but voluntary emigration; it set its face against all ideas of emigration by compulsion. But the House must consider, that if the distress and misery among the people were such as the evidence stated, very little persuasion, much less compulsion, would be necessary ... They would be glad to accept of any terms offered to them for removing from scenes of destitution at home, to those of comparative comfort in the colonies ...

(William Horton MP, *Parliamentary Debates*, xviii, 939–950, March, 1828)

Source 4.13 *Edward Gibbon Wakefield's ideas of 'Systematic Colonisation'*

On the whole, emigration promised to be of very little service until Mr Wakefield promulgated [made known] the theory of colonization which goes by his name; and suggested two simple expedients [ideas] ... These suggestions consisted in putting a stop to the gratuitous [free] disposal of the waste lands of the colonies, and selling them at a certain uniform price ... and in making a selection of young persons of both sexes out of those who were desirous of being so assisted to emigrate.... This change in the character of colonization ... makes colonization, indeed, an extension of civilized society, instead of that mere emigration which aimed at little more than shovelling out your paupers to where they might die ...

(Charles Buller MP, *Parliamentary Debates*, lxviii, 513, 522, April 1843)

Numbers of Emigrants

Emigration had been an important factor in the late eighteenth century but in the nineteenth century it increased dramatically.

Source 4.14 *Total emigration from the British Isles 1815–54*

1815–19	97 799
1820–24	95 030
1825–29	121 084
1830–34	381 956
1835–39	287 358
1840–44	465 577
1845–49	1 029 209
1850–54	1 638 945

Source 4.15 *Destination of emigrants from the British Isles*

	Canada	USA	Australia & New Zealand	South Africa	Elsewhere
1821	12 995	4 958	320	No	384
1831	58 067	23 418	1 561	figures	114
1841	38 164	45 017	32 625	until	2 786
1851	42 605	267 357	21 532	1881	4 472

Source 4.16 *Advertisement for an emigrant ship*

FOR PICTOU DIRECT
The Fine Brigantine
GOOD INTENT
220 Tons Burden
E. HIBBARD, Supercargo

will be ready to sail from Aberdeen in March, and intends calling at Cromarty about the end of that month, if a sufficient number of passengers offer.

This Vessel has most excellent accommodation for Passengers, and Mr Hibbard, the Supercargo, will pay every attention.

•The fares are as follows, and payable at going on board:

Cabin passengers	10 guineas each
Steerage ditto	7 guineas each
Ditto, from 7 to 14 years old	5 guineas each
Ditto, from 2 to 7 years old	3 guineas each
Infants go free	

Source 4.17   Section of an emigrant sship, the *Bourneuf.*

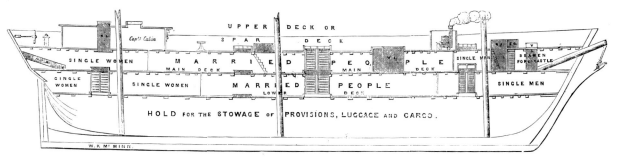

SECTION OF THE EMIGRANT SHIP "BOURNEUF," OF LIVERPOOL, BURDEN 1495 TONS; SHOWING THE ARRANGEMENT FOR GOVERNMENT PASSENGERS TO AUSTRALIA.

Source 4.18   The emigrant is shown a berth, a shelf of coarse pinewood in a noisome [disgusting] dungeon, airless and lightless, in which several hundred persons of both sexes and all ages are stowed away, on shelves two feet one inch [62 cm] above each other, three feet [90 cm] wide and six feet [1.8 m] long, still reeking from the ineradicable stench left by the emigrants on the last voyage . . . Still he believes that the plank is his own, and only finds when the anchor is up that he must share his six feet three, with a bedfellow. He finds that cleanliness is impossible, that no attempt is made to purify the reeking den into which he has been thrust, and that the thirty days voyage he has been promised will not, from the rotteness of the rigging and the unsoundness of the hull, be completed in less than sixty . . . After a few days have been spent in the pestilential atmosphere created by the festering mass of squalid humanity imprisoned between the damp and steaming decks, the scourge bursts out, and to the miseries of filth, foul air and darkness is added the Cholera. Amid hundreds of men, women and children, dressing and undressing, washing, quarrelling, fighting, cooking and drinking, one hears the groans and screams of a patient in the last agonies of this plague.

(*The Times*, 1854)

Source 4.19   Before the emigrant has been a week at sea he is an altered man. How can it be otherwise? Hundreds of poor people, men, women, and children, of all ages from the drivelling idiot of 90 to the babe just born, huddled together, without light, without air, wallowing in filth, and breathing a fetid atmosphere, sick in body, dispirited in heart; the fevered patients lying between the sound, in sleeping places so narrow as almost to deny them the power of indulging, by a change of position, the natural restlessness of the disease; living without food or medicine except as administered by the hand of casual charity; dying without the voice of spiritual consolation, and buried in the deep without the rites of the Church. The food is generally ill-selected, and seldom sufficiently cooked . . . The supply of water, hardly enough for cooking and drinking, does not allow washing. In many ships the filthy beds, teeming with all abominations, are never required to be brought on deck and aired; the narrow space between the sleeping berths and the piles of boxes is never washed or scraped, until the day before arrival, when all hands are required to 'scrub up' and put on a fair face for the doctor and Government inspector. No moral restraint is attempted; the voice of prayer is never heard; drunkeness, with its consequent train of ruffianly debasement, is not discouraged, because it is profitable to the captain who traffics [deals] in the grog.

In the ship which brought me out from London last April, the passengers were found in provisions by the owners, according to a contract . . . The meat was of the worst quality. The supply of water shipped on board was abundant, but the quantity served out to the passengers was so scanty that they were frequently obliged to throw overboard their salt provisions and rice (a most important article of their food), because they had not water enough both for the necessary cooking, and the satisfying of their raging thirst afterwards.

They could only afford water for washing by withdrawing it from the cooking of their food. No cleanliness was enforced; the beds never aired; the master during the whole voyage never entered the steerage, and would listen to no complaints; the dietary contracted for was, with some exceptions, nominally supplied, though at irregular periods; but false measures were used (in which the water and several articles of dry food were served), the gallon measure containing but three quarts, which fact I proved in Quebec, and had the captain fined for . . .

The case of this ship was not one of peculiar misconduct, on the contrary, I have the strongest reason to know from information which I have received from very many emigrants well-known to me who came over this year in different vessels, that this ship was better regulated and more comfortable than many that reached Canada . . .

(Letter from Stephen de Vere to T. F. Elliott, 30 Nov. 1847 in *Parliamentary Papers*, XLVII, pp. 13–14)

Source 4.20 Fever on board ship

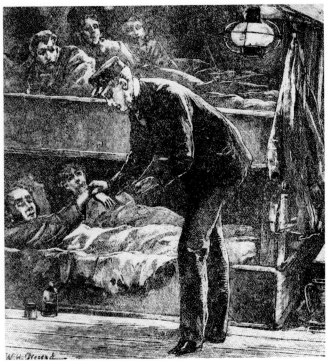

Using the Evidence
---

1. Look at sources 4.12 and 4.13.
   (a) What are Wakefield's two suggestions?
   (b) In what ways are the ideas put forward in 4.12 different from those of Wakefield?
   (c) Why would Wakefield not have approved of the scenes described in 4.5?

2. In source 4.15, study the figures for emigration to Canada, USA and Australia and New Zealand. Describe the differences which appear between 1821 and 1851.

3. From source 4.16, give examples which show that this advertisement was meant to attract customers.

4. Look at sources 4.18 and 4.19.
   (a) What purpose do you think lay behind the publication of these accounts?
   (b) What evidence is there in 4.19 that the captain was dishonest?

Source 4.21 Emigrants Departing

Coursework

Empathy

Form groups of 3 to 4 and study sources 4.16 to 4.21. You are to imagine that you are members of a government committee required to draw up a bill to improve conditions on emigrant ships. Make sure your recommendations can be made to work, so that dishonest captains like the one in 4.19 cannot simply ignore them while at sea.

On the Road

Crossing a River

The Second Season

The First Season

In the New World

Apart from all the 'pushes' and 'pulls' of emigration, those who had already settled in the New World needed others to help them settle the new land. Shipping companies were also keen to encourage emigration. Advertisements were issued stressing the fertility of the soil and the good life. These claims were often greatly exaggerated. As an American, Joseph Tucker, wrote in the late eighteenth century 'a man may possess twenty miles square in this glorious Country, and not be able to get a Dinner.' But once people had sold all to make the journey to the New World it was often impossibly difficult for them to return home.

Source 4.23 The Emigrant's Dream

Source 4.24 *Another view of the 'Promised Land'*
We would bring them to the emigrant sheds at Quebec or Montreal, and we could tell them that during the last great emigration hundreds, we might say thousands, died in these sheds of a fearful pestilence. We would bring them to Cape Breton or the district around Pictou in Nova Scotia, and we suspect we could point out an amount of destitution among old settlers not to be outdone by that of the Hebrides . . .

(The Witness)

Emigration from Ireland

The peasants of Ireland were poorer than anywhere else in the British Isles. There was very little industry in Ireland so the rapidly growing population were all dependent on the

land for their livelihood. The most productive crop from their small landholdings was potatoes. By the nineteenth century most of the population of Ireland relied solely on the potato for their survival. In 1845 and then succeeding years, disaster struck.

Source 4.25 *The Potato Blight*
Belfast, 18 October 1845
Potatoes!
Read – For the sake of the country Read . . . No man can stop the disease; nor can any man be certain that a single tuber will remain in the island at the end of a few months! In this lies the terrific danger – the RISK is absolutely appalling. *Two thirds* at least of the peasantry have nothing – absolutely NOTHING, to depend upon for existence save the potatoes . . . If their potatoes decay they must die by the Million.

(Letter to the Duke of Wellington, W. Mss.)

Source 4.26 *Letter from an Irish Peasant to his parents in America*
Now my dear father and mother, if you knew what hunger we and our fellow-countrymen are suffering, you would take us out of this poverty Isle. We can only say, the scourge of God fell down on Ireland in taking away the potatoes, they being the only support of the people. So dear father and mother, if you don't endeavour to take us out of it, it will be the first news you will hear by some friend of me and my little family to be lost by hunger, and there are thousands dread they will share the same fate.

(Letter from Michael Rush of Ardglass, quoted in P. F. Speed, *The Potato Famine and the Irish Emigrants*, Longman (Then and There series) p. 63)

Source 4.27 *Population of Ireland, 1811–51* (millions)

1811–5.96	1841–8.20
1821–6.80	1851–6.51
1831–7.77	

Source 4.28 Irish Peasants searching for potatoes

_____ **Using the Evidence** _____

1. Study sources 4.22 to 4.24. You are a destitute farm labourer in Britain. Which of these views of the New World are you going to accept? Give reasons for your answer.

2. Use sources 4.25, 4.26 and 4.28 to explain why the potato blight led to emigration from Ireland.

3. Look at source 4.27.
   (a) Work out roughly what Ireland's population would have been in 1851 if the famine had not occurred.
   (b) As many as a million people may have died as a result of the famine. Roughly how many emigrated then?
   (You can learn more about the Potato Famine in Ireland by reading the book quoted from in 4.26 – P. F. Speed, *The Potato Famine and the Irish Emigrants*.)

Case Study – the Causes of Emigration from the Highlands

We have seen that one powerful cause of emigration was the effect of changes in the way the land was used. One area that was greatly affected by such changes was the Highlands of Scotland. Formerly, the clan chiefs there had encouraged a large population, to make their clan more powerful. By the mid-eighteenth century, however, clans were no longer fighting units. The chiefs now looked upon themselves as landowners, and wanted to live wealthy lives like landowners elsewhere. To do so, they would need to get more money from their estates, and this meant higher rents from the tenants living there.

Most landowners discovered the solution was not that simple. The changes in the Highlands which they helped to bring about are generally referred to as the Highland Clearances. Using the sources in the next few pages you are going to investigate to what extent the Clearances can be blamed for the large-scale emigration from the Highlands in the nineteenth century. Most of the evidence given here refers to the county of Sutherland in the extreme north-west of Scotland. At that time, most of Sutherland was owned by the Countess of Sutherland, who was thus the biggest landowner in Britain. Her husband was the Marquis of Stafford (later, Duke of Sutherland), who was the wealthiest man in Britain.

The Highland problem

Source 4.29 The proprietors [landowners] find their lands over-stocked with people, who are mere cumberers of the soil, eat up its produce, and prevent its improvement, without being able to afford a rent nearly adequate to that which should be afforded . . . were their fields under proper management.

(James Anderson, *An Account of the Present State of the Hebrides*, 1785 p. 25)

Source 4.30 Every family has a small farm which they are too poor to stock with sheep or cattle, and in a bad year, as the last, when all the Oats were spoilt with the rain, they were reduced to absolute starvation. I have seen misery in Wales, but till I came into this Country, I had no idea of human or indeed any other Creatures existing in such habitations as I have seen, and their food, if possible, still worse.

(R. Leighton (ed) *Correspondence of Charlotte Grenville, Lady Williams Wynn* 1920, p. 127)

The landowners' answer – the Sutherland Plan

Source 4.31 As there was every reason therefore for concluding, that the mountainous parts of the estate, and indeed, of the county of SUTHERLAND, were as much calculated for the maintenance of stock as they were unfit for the habitation of man, there could be no doubt as to the propriety of converting them into sheep walks, *provided* the people could be at the same time, settled in situations, where, by the exercise of their honest industry, they could obtain a decent livelihood. . .

It had long been known, that the coast of SUTHERLAND abounded with many different kinds of fish, not only sufficient for the consumption of the country, but affording also, a supply *to any extent*, for more distant markets. . .

It seemed as if it had been pointed out by Nature, that the system for this remote district . . . was, to convert the mountainous districts into sheep-walks, and to remove the inhabitants to the coast. . .

(James Loch, *An Account of the Improvements on the Estates of the Marquess of Stafford*, 1820)

Source 4.32 A system commenced in this country about the year 1807, which has been followed out extensively. As the interior of the country consisted mainly of moor grounds covered with heath, the proprietors were convinced that these grounds could be more profitably laid out in sheep-walks, than (as formerly) in the rearing of black cattle. With this view, the interior was let to sheep-farmers, and the tenantry were removed to the coast . . . Lairg being an inland parish, this circumstance accounts for the great decrease in its population.

(*New Statistical Account of Scotland*, 1845, vol. XV, p. 62 (parish of Lairg))

Source 4.33 Population change in Sutherland, 1801–31

PARISH	1801	1811	1821	1831
Assynt	2395	2479	2803	3161
Clyne	1643	1639	1874	1711
Creich	1974	1969	2354	2562
Dornoch	2362	2681	3100	3380
Durness	1208	1155	1004	1153
Eddrachillies	1253	1147	1229	1965
Farr	2408	2408	1994	2073
Golspie	1616	1391	1036	1149
Kildonan	1440	1574	565	257
Lairg	1209	1354	1094	1045
Loth	1374	1330	2008	2214
Reay	865	861	1057	1013
Rogart	2022	2148	1986	1805
Tongue	1348	1493	1736	2030

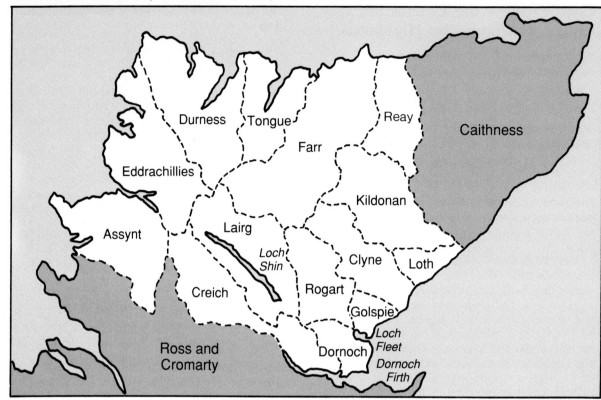

The Sutherland Plan in action

According to James Loch in 4.31, the Sutherland Plan was meant to benefit the ordinary tenants. If this actually happened, we would not expect them to emigrate.

Source 4.35 *James Loch's account of the evictions*
Some of the people, however, in 1819, were impressed with the notion that if they resumed possession of their holdings, they would be able to retain them for another year, and that something might happen during that period, to prevent the arrangement taking place. In this view, they retired upon the approach of the sheriff's officers, taking with them all their goods; but as soon as the constables left the glen, they re-appeared, and constructed new, or repaired their old turf huts, and re-occupied their former possessions. It rendered a second ejectment necessary . . . It further made it necessary for the local management to adopt some measure to prevent the possibility of its repetition . . .; this was to be accomplished either by removing, or by destroying the [roof] timber.

. . . the local management adopted the only course which could be pursued – that was, to collect and burn it. . . This simple and necessary act . . . has been falsified in every possible way . . .

(Loch, pp. 91–3)

Source 4.36 *Rev. Donald Sage's account of the evictions*
It was in the month of April 1819 . . .
At an early hour on a Tuesday, Mr Sellar, escorted by a large body of constables, sheriff-officers and others, commenced work . . . They gave the inmates half an hour to pack up and carry off their furniture and then set the cottages on fire. To this plan they ruthlessly adhered. The roofs and rafters were lighted up into one red blaze.

(Donald Sage, *Memorabilia Domestica*, 1889, p. 215)

Source 4.37 *Donald Macleod's account of the evictions*
I was an eye-witness of the scene. This calamity came on the people quite unexpectedly. Strong parties, for each district, rushed on the dwellings of this devoted people, and immediately commenced setting fire to them . . . The consternation and confusion were extreme; little or no time was given for removal of persons or property – the people striving to remove the sick and the helpless before the fire should reach them – next, struggling to remove the most valuable of their effects.

(Donald Macleod, *Gloomy Memories*, 1892 ed., p. 16)

The coastal settlements

According to the Sutherland Plan, the people cleared from the interior were to settle in fishing villages on the coast. After being evicted from their homes, however, some people moved away from the area altogether – to the factory towns of Central Scotland and England, or abroad, to Canada or the United States. Some people did stay on the lots provided for them on the coast.

Source 4.38 *The view of the West Coast factor* (factor = estate manager). The new lotters in Rhue Stoer appear contented and reconciled to their change – the young men who were never at sea before Whitsunday 1819 are now constantly engaged in fishing, and some of them are preparing to go to Caithness. . .

(Quoted in Eric Richards, *A History of the Highland Clearances I – Agrarian Transformation and the Evictions*, Croom Helm, 1982, p. 340)

Source 4.39 For a few, some miserable patches of ground along the shore were doled as lots without anything in the shape of the poorest hut to shelter them. Upon these lots it was decided that they should build houses at their own expense, and cultivate the ground, at the same time occupying them-selves as fishermen, although the great majority of them had never set foot in a boat in their lives.

(Rev. Donald Sage, *Memorabilia Domestica*, p. 215)

Source 4.40 *Rev. David Mackenzie's criticisms*
From what I have heard and seen of the quality of land which can be given them according to the new arrangements, it will not produce of Corn what will support their families for half a year; and being totally ignorant of sea faring, their supplies from the Ocean must be scanty and precarious during the storms of winter and spring.

I candidly submit to you, with all deference, I am persuaded that the great population to be removed at Whitsunday 1819 from the upper parts, to the sea coast of the Parish, cannot, if left to depend for subsistence on the production of their Stances, have a comfortable living, and from this persuasion I cannot attempt to convince the people that the change will be for their advantage.

(Quoted in Richards, p. 321)

Source 4.41 *Rev. Hugh Mackenzie's criticisms*
In these places the land, already occupied by a few, but now divided among many, was totally inadequate to the maintenance of all, and fishing became their necessary resource. And thus, on a tempestuous [stormy] coast, with no harbours but such as nature

provided . . . were these people often necessitated to plunge into debt for providing fishing materials, and to encounter dangers, immensely increased by their unavoidable ignorance of navigation, in order to obtain subsistence and defray [raise money for] their rents.

(*New Statistical Account of Scotland*, 1845, vol. XV, p. 185 (parish of Tongue)).

Source 4.42 *Donald Macleod's accusation*
Every means were resorted to, to discourage the people, and to persuade them to give up their hold-ings quietly, and quit the country; and to those who could not be induced [persuaded] to do so, scraps of moor and bog land were offered . . ., on which it was next to impossible to exist, in order that they may be scared into going entirely away.

(Donald Macleod, p. 5)

Source 4.43 *James Loch's policy*
I am particularly anxious that their lots should be so small as to prevent their massing any considerable part of their rent by selling a beast, their rent must not depend on that. In short I wish them to become fishers only, but if you give them any extent of land . . . they will never embark heartily in that pursuit.

(Quoted in Richards, pp. 318–19)

Source 4.44 *James Loch sums up*
It is no doubt true, that if the same plans were again to be executed [carried out], many mistakes might be avoided . . . But this much is asserted, that whatever mistakes may have been committed . . . there has never been at any period, while these changes were going on, a want of consideration and attention to the interests, the feelings, and the prejudices of the people . . .

Not an individual has left the estate, who might have remained on it if he had wished. . .

(Loch, pp. 168–9)

Famine and emigration

By the 1830s it was clear that the Sutherland Plan had failed. People had been cleared from the interior and those who remained in Sutherland were crowded along the coast. For reasons shown above, many were unable to take up fishing as an occupation, while other new industries such as the coal mine at Brora had also failed. The people were forced to rely on their small plots of land for survival – the one thing James Loch (4.43) had been determined to prevent. As in Ireland, the basic crop was potatoes, and like Ireland, disaster struck the potato crop in the 1840s. Although the Duke of Sutherland spent £18 000 on food for his tenants, there was now open recognition of a change in official attitude to emigration.

Source 4.45 *Importance of the potato*
Those who are habitually and entirely fed on potatoes live upon the extreme verge of human subsistence, and when they are deprived of their accustomed food there is nothing cheaper to which they can resort. They have already reached the lowest point of the descending scale, and there is nothing beyond but starvation and beggary.

(C. E. Trevelyan, *The Irish Crisis*, 1848, p. 9)

Source 4.46 *Effects of the potato failure*
Such was the terror inspired by potato disease, that numbers of the crofters came to me and expressed the opinion that the sooner they left the country and emigrated to America the better for them, and asking me to recommend the Duke to assist them to go ... and the consequence was that in the three following years nearly a thousand people emigrated, principally to Upper Canada and Cape Breton; an immense blessing for most of those who went, and a valuable relief in the various parishes of this district ... which had become overcrowded and populous ... Five large ships from Liverpool were engaged ... The cost of this emigration amounted to about £7000, and it was well expended money.

(Evander MacIver, *Memoirs of a Highland Gentleman*, 1905, p. 62)

Source 4.47 *The view of Patrick Sellar* (sheep-farmer responsible for many evictions)
If facilities were given for emigration, there would be a general wish to get abroad. The *difference in cost* of eating Indian corn in America, besides eating it at home would pay the expense of their transport. Ten millions spent in applying the remedy would be a profitable remedy, but ten millions applied, merely to pass through the Bowels of a misgoverned people is worse than thrown away. It destroys their self-reliance – makes them a mistletoe on the British oak.

(Quoted in Eric Richards, *A History of the Highland Clearances* II – *Emigration, Protests, Reasons*, Croom Helm, 1985, p. 402)

Source 4.48 *The aims of the Highlands and Islands Emigration Society*
... to procure help for those who wish to emigrate but have not the means of doing so, to afford information, encouragement and assistance to all whom emigration would be a relief from want and misery ...

That you should feel pain in leaving your own country is natural, ... but is the sacrifice of this feeling which emigration demands peculiar to you? Remember the families that were most respected in this country twenty years ago. How many of them have gone abroad? Is it harder for you to leave your native land than it was for them? They have subdued the feeling of pain, and so ought you, for you have stronger reasons for emigrating than they had.

We will do what we can to assist you, and we will endeavour to procure assistance for you from others ...

(Quoted in John Prebble, *The Highland Clearances*, Penguin edition, 1969, pp. 201–2)

Leaving the Highlands

By the 1840s the government, landowners and charitable organizations were openly encouraging Highlanders to emigrate. Landowners who previously had seemed determined to keep their tenants now paid to have them removed. The Clearances shattered the Highlanders' belief in their chiefs. They had been evicted from land which they had occupied since time immemorial. They could not believe that their landowners could prefer sheep to men. Many Highland emigrants carried with them bitter memories:

Source 4.49 *A Highland Bard looks back*
Chorus Mo mhallachd aig na caoraich mhor
    Cait' bheil clann nan daoine coir?
    Dhealaich rium nuair bha mi og
    Man robh Duthaich 'c Aoidh 'na fasach.

1. Tha tri fichead bliadhn's a tri
   On a dh'fhàg sinn Duthaich Mhic Aoidh.
   Cait' bheil gillean glan mo chridh
   'S na nighneagan cho boidheach?

2. Ceud Diuc Chataibh le cuid foill
   'S le chuid cairdeas do na Goill,
   Gum b'ann an Iutharn' 'n robh a shail
   'S gum b'fhearr leam Iudas lamh rium.

3. O mo mhallachd air an sguad
   A chuir Clann Mhic Aoidh fo ruaig
   On a mhonadh gus a'chuan
   Gun tigh, gun bual, gun chro ac'.

Chorus My curses on the great sheep,
    Where are the children of the fine people
    That I was separated from when I was young
    Before the Mackay country was deserted?

1. It is sixty-three years
   Since we left the Mackay country
   Where are the fine young men dear to me
   Or the girls who were so pretty?

2. O first Duke of Sutherland, with your
        share of treachery
    And your friendship to the foreigners
    It was in Hell that your heels were
    And I'd prefer to have Judas alongside
        me.

3. O my curse on the squad
    That routed the Mackay clan
    From the moorland to the sea
    Without house, fold or cattle.

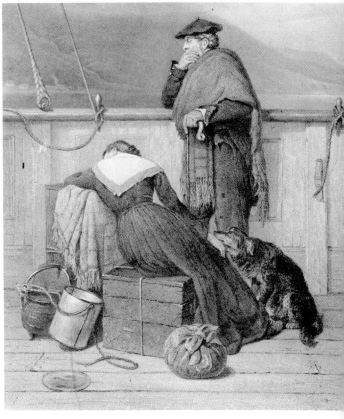

Source 4.50 Lochaber No More (John Watson
Nicol)

Source 4.51 The Last of the Clan (Thomas Faed)

Using the Evidence

1. Study sources 4.29 and 4.30. From the point of view of an improving landlord, anxious for more rent – what was the 'Highland problem'?

2. Using sources 4.31 and 4.32, explain how the Sutherland Plan was meant to benefit i) the landowner ii) the ordinary people.

3. Study sources 4.32, 4.33 and 4.34.
   (a) How do you account for the change in Lairg parish's population?
   (b) What connection might there be between the changes shown for the parishes of Kildonan and Loth?
   (c) Why are sources 4.33 and 4.34 not adequate for firmly stating what the reason was for population change in any parish? Why are they particularly inadequate for a big parish like Farr?

4. Study sources 4.35 to 4.37 after you have considered these facts:
   (i) James Loch (4.35) was advisor to the Marquis of Stafford, the owner of the estate;
   (ii) Donald Macleod (4.37) wrote his account 20 years after the events he described, after he himself had been evicted.
   (a) Explain how the evidence in 4.35 and 4.37 might be influenced by the background of the writer in each case.
   (b) Which view are you going to accept? Justify your choice.

5. Study source 4.38. Why might this writer want to give the impression that the people on the coast were contented? Find a word or phrase which suggests that he realises the people are not entirely happy.

6. Look at sources 4.39 to 4.42.
   (a) What problems were there with the pieces of land on the coast?
   (b) How did Donald Macleod account for these conditions?

7. Read source 4.43 carefully. Do you think James Loch could have succeeded with his main aim mentioned here? Use sources 4.38 to 4.41 to build up as detailed an answer as possible.

8. Sources 4.46 to 4.48 sum up the views of the landed classes to emigration. What was the most important reason for these classes encouraging the poor to emigrate? Was it:
   (a) They genuinely wanted to help the people and thought they would be better off abroad;
   (b) They thought the people left at home would be better off if some emigrated;
   (c) They thought the people were a burden to them and their estates would be better if some people left.

9. (a) Describe the different feelings expressed by the poet in source 4.49. For example, compare v. 1 with v. 2 and 3.
   (b) This poet died in 1895. Why do you think his poem has survived?

10. Take sources 4.50 and 4.51 in turn. Explain what point each artist is trying to make, and give examples from each painting to illustrate your answers.

Coursework

Cause and Effect

Re-read source 4.44. By the time James Loch had written this, several thousand people had left Sutherland. For this piece of work, you must draw together all your conclusions relating to the evictions (4.35–4.38) and the coastal settlements (4.39–4.44). Was Loch right when he said that no one had been made to leave Sutherland against his wishes?

5 The Railways

The Industrial Revolution had led to the growth of factories and towns. These changes could not have taken place without the development of a good transport system at the same time. Raw materials and finished products had to be moved quickly and cheaply; letters and other news needed rapid delivery; the growing towns required daily supplies of food; and people too, needed a safe and comfortable means of transport. It is not surprising, therefore, that the Industrial Revolution was accompanied by a transport revolution.

The first response to these needs was the introduction of turnpike roads. Under this system, travellers paid to pass over a certain stretch of road, and the money so earned was

The Railway Station (William Powell Frith)

used to improve and repair the road. These improvements made possible the stage-coach age. Companies established networks throughout the different regions and competed fiercely with each other for passengers.

Industrialisation, however, required the movement of heavy and bulky goods such as coal, iron-ore and raw cotton. Transporting these by road was difficult and expensive. Thus the canal system developed in the last 30 years of the eighteenth century. It was the canals that really made the Industrial Revolution possible by providing a cheap and convenient means of carrying these heavy industrial goods; but as industry expanded at an ever greater rate, it became clear that canals, too, had their shortcomings. They were expensive to build and maintain, and simply too slow for the mass production of the new machine age.

Already some mine owners used horse-drawn wagons on wooden rails to transport coal. Soon iron rails were being used, with stationary steam engines to pull wagons up the steeper hills. By the beginning of the nineteenth century several engineers were trying to produce a locomotive: a steam engine which could pull wagons along the track behind it. The most important of these engineers were Richard Trevithick, a Cornishman, Richard Blenkinsop, a colliery engineer from Leeds, and George Stephenson, a young engineer from Northumberland.

Source 5.1 Horse-drawn wagons (a detail from a *Stockton and Darlington Share Certificate*, 1823)

Source 5.2 *Horse- and steam-power*
Horses or steam engines are used to haul waggons up a slope. In Wales, where small waggons are commonly used, horses are employed to pull waggons up hills. The laden waggons are coupled together and a single horse pulls a number of them. But when a hill is reached the horse hauls only one waggon up at a time. When all the waggons are at the top, they are coupled together again and one horse pulls all of them. If the hill is very long or steep – and this does occur in the Newcastle district – a steam engine is installed at the top of the hill and the waggons are hauled up by means of a cable.

(Louis de Gallois, *Report on English Railways*, 1818)

Source 5.3 *A Blenkinsop locomotive at work*
At Leeds they have been daily at work for some time back leading their Coals in this way and as their Road is perfectly level their Engines take with great ease 24, twenty Boll wagons loaded at a time – each wagon weighs with its contents about 3½ Tons [3.5 t] making together an aggregate weight of 84 Tons [85 t]. When the Machine is lightly loaded it can be propelled at the rate of 10 Miles [16 km an hour]; but when properly loaded is calculated to go at the rate from 3½ to 4 miles [5.5 to 6.5 km] an hour upon a level way . . .

. . . I have no doubt that an immense saving will be made by the adoption of Mr Blenkinsop's new method . . .

(Charles Brandling's 'Letter Book' (private collection of P. Burgoyne Johnson) in J. Addy and E. G. Power (eds), *The Industrial Revolution*, Then and There Sourcebook)

Source 5.4 Richard Trevithick's Catch-Me-Who-Can (T. P. Rowlandson)

George Stephenson saw the great possibilities for Trevithick's engine, and worked to find an improved design. He became engineer on a newly planned railway between Stockton and Darlington where he persuaded the owner to use locomotive power. The Stockton and Darlington railway was opened in 1825 and was the first public railway in the world to use locomotive power over part of its length.

Source 5.5 The Opening of the Stockton and Darlington Railway (J. R. Brown)

THE
STOCKTON & DARLINGTON
RAILWAY COMPANY
Hereby give Notice,

THAT the FORMAL OPENING of their RAILWAY will take place on the 27th instant, as announced in the public Papers.—The Proprietors will assemble at the Permanent Steam Engine, situated below BRUSSELTON TOWER*, about nine Miles West of DARLINGTON, at 8 o'clock, and, after examining their extensive inclined Planes there, will start from the Foot of the BRUSSELTON descending Plane, at 9 o'clock, in the following Order :——

    1. THE COMPANY's LOCOMOTIVE ENGINE.
    2. The ENGINE's TENDER, with Water and Coals.
    3. SIX WAGGONS, laden with Coals, Merchandize, &c.
    4. The COMMITTEE, and other PROPRIETORS, in the COACH belonging to the COMPANY.
    5. SIX WAGGONS, with Seats reserved for STRANGERS.
    6. FOURTEEN WAGGONS, for the Conveyance of Workmen and others.

    ☞ The WHOLE of the above to proceed to STOCKTON.

    7. SIX WAGGONS, laden with Coals, to leave the Procession at the DARLINGTON BRANCH.
    8. SIX WAGGONS, drawn by Horses, for Workmen and others.
    9. Ditto   Ditto.
    10. Ditto   Ditto.
    11. Ditto   Ditto.

The COMPANY's WORKMEN to leave the Procession at DARLINGTON, and DINE at that Place at ONE o'clock; excepting those to whom Tickets are specially given for YARM, and for whom Conveyances will be provided, on their Arrival at STOCKTON.

TICKETS will be given to the Workmen who are to dine at DARLINGTON, specifying the Houses of Entertainment.

The PROPRIETORS, and such of the NOBILITY and GENTRY as may honour them with their Company, will DINE precisely at THREE o'clock, at the TOWN-HALL, STOCKTON.—Such of the Party as may incline to return to DARLINGTON that Evening, will find Conveyances in waiting for their Accommodation, to start from the COMPANY's WHARF there precisely at SEVEN o'clock.

The COMPANY take this Opportunity of enjoining on all their WORK-PEOPLE that Attention to *Sobriety* and *Decorum* which they have hitherto had the Pleasure of observing.

The COMMITTEE give this PUBLIC NOTICE, that all Persons who shall ride upon, or by the sides of, the RAILWAY, on Horseback, will incur the Penalties imposed by the Acts of Parliament passed relative to this RAILWAY.

* Any Individuals desirous of seeing the Train of Waggons descending the inclined Plane from ETHERLEY, and in Progress to BRUSSELTON, may have an Opportunity of so doing, by being on the Railway at ST. HELEN's AUCKLAND not later than Half-past Seven o'clock.

RAILWAY-OFFICE, *Sept. 19th, 1825.*

ATKINSON's Office, High Row, Darlington

1. Look at sources 5.1 and 5.2. What evidence is there that:
   (a) horse-drawn transport was slow;
   (b) in some cases steam-drawn transport was better?

2. What is the main advantage for the system described in source 5.3, compared with those in sources 5.1 and 5.2?

3. Look at source 5.4.
   (a) Describe fully what is happening.
   (b) How does it show that this was a completely new form of transport?
   (c) How useful do you find this source as a way of showing what people thought of the new invention?

4. From sources 5.5 and 5.6, find all the evidence you can which show that people regarded the opening of the Stockton and Darlington Railway as a very special occasion.

The Liverpool and Manchester Railway

Source 5.7 *Proposal for a new means of transport*
At this period (1824) an effort was made by the Liverpool merchants to have a railway between Manchester and Liverpool, the expense and delays of the canal navigation having become intolerable.

George Stephenson had been employed on the Stockton and Darlington Railway, which was then in progress, and was engaged for the Liverpool and Manchester line . . .

(Joseph Mitchell, *Reminiscences of my Life in the Highlands*, 1833, p. 101)

Source 5.8 *Reasons for the new railway*
The total quantity of goods passing between Liverpool and Manchester is at least one thousand tons a day. The bulk of this merchandise is carried, either by the Duke of Bridgewater's Canal, or by the Mersey and Irwell navigation. By both these means goods must pass up the river Mersey, a distance of 16 or 18 miles, subject to serious delays from contrary winds, and quite often to actual damage or loss from storms. The average length of passage may be taken at 36 hours, longer or shorter according to the state of the winds and tides. The average charge upon goods, for the last fourteen years, has been about 15 shillings [75 p] a ton.

By the planned Rail-road, the transport of goods between Liverpool and Manchester will be carried out in four or five hours, and the charge to the merchant will be reduced by at least one third.

But it is not altogether on account of the high charges of the water carriers that a Rail-road is desireable. The Canals are unable to carry goods regularly and punctually at all periods and seasons. In summer time there is often a shortage of water, obliging boats to go only half-loaded. In winter they are sometimes locked up with frosts for weeks together. From these problems a Rail-road would be altogether free. There is still another ground of objection to the present system of carriage by Canals, namely, the pilfering for which the privacy of such a roundabout and lengthy journey gives so many opportunities. Whereas, carriage by Railway, done in a few hours and where every delay must be accounted for, will have much of the publicity and, as a result, the safety of the King's highways.

(*Prospectus of the Liverpool and Manchester Rail-Road Company*, 1824 – a prospectus is a document by which businessmen try to persuade people to buy shares in a company.)

Source 5.9 By the establishment of a rail-way, the inhabitants of Liverpool will be entitled to buy their coals several shillings per ton below the price which they now pay. By opening the collieries to the sea, Liverpool will become one of the greatest shipping ports for coal in the kingdom. A railroad will facilitate [make easier] the conveyance of this indispensable article, together with the agricultural produce, the iron, limestone, etc., throughout the whole manufacturing districts of Lancashire . . .

(*Quarterly Review*, 1825, vol. 31, p. 375)

Source 5.10 I find all my friends Railway mad . . . and I firmly believe from what I see that though the great part of the present agitation arises from ill-favoured expectation and skilful manoeuvres of persons who mean to prosper by the rage, yet I am satisfied that there is a general demand for an additional means of transport which must be met in some way or other.

(Letter from James Loch (1824) quoted in Eric Richards, *The Leviathan of Wealth – The Sutherland Fortune in the Industrial Revolution*, 1973, pp. 56–7. James Loch was the adviser to the Marquis of Stafford, who received all the profits from the Bridgewater Canal at this time.)

Source 5.11 Liverpool – Manchester area

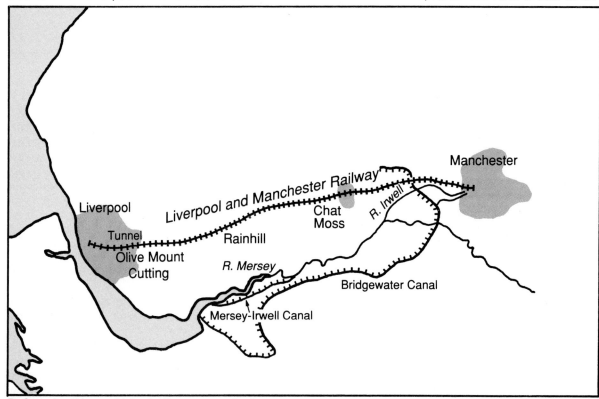

says we will have a hundred men against us. The Company thinks the Great men have no right to stop a survey.

(Letters of George Stephenson, Liverpool Public Library, in Richards, *Leviathan of Wealth*, p. 55)

Source 5.13 When the bill went into committee [in Parliament] the opposition was strong and severe . . . Mr Stephenson was attacked with an undeserving severity; the claims of the land-owner were placed in a prominent position; the locomotive was laughed at, the speed was denied . . .

Vegetation, it was prophesied, would cease wherever the locomotive passed. The value of land would be lowered by it; the market gardener would be ruined by it . . . Steam would vanish before storm and frost; property would be deteriorated near a station . . . it was erroneous, impracticable, unjust. It was a great and scandalous attack on private property, upon public grounds.

(J. Francis *A History of the English Railway*, 1851, vol. I, pp. 106–7)

Before the line could be built, a survey had to be carried out, and a Bill had to pass through Parliament giving permission. Opponents to the railway used both of these as opportunities to try to stop the railway.

Source 5.12 We have had sad work with Lord Derby, Lord Sefton and Bradshaw the Great Canal Proprietor, whose grounds we go through with the projected Railway. Their ground is blockaded on every side to prevent us getting on with the survey. Bradshaw fired guns through his ground in the course of the night to prevent the Surveyors getting on in the dark . . . the Liverpool Railway Company are determined to force a Survey if possible. Lord Sefton

Source 5.14 No engineer in his senses would go through Chat Moss if he wanted to make a railroad from Liverpool to Manchester . . . In the centre, where this railroad is to cross, it is all pulp from the top to the depth of 34 feet [10 m]; at 34 feet there is a vein of 4 or 6 inches [10 or 15 cm] of clay; below

that there are 2 or 3 feet [60 or 90 cm] of quicksand;
and the bottom of that is hard clay, which keeps all
the water in.

(Evidence to the Parliamentary Committee, quoted in:
S. Smiles, *The Story of the Life of George
Stephenson*, pp. 169–70)

Building the Liverpool and Manchester railway

The main problems in building the line were
Chat Moss, a great bog, described above; a
tunnel 2 km in length on the outskirts of
Liverpool; and the nearby Olive Mount Cutting,
30 m deep.

Source 5.15 Excavation at Olive Mount, about
1828

Source 5.16 View of the Railway Across Chat
Moss, 1831

Source 5.17 Chat Moss is a huge Bog – in some places 30 to 35 feet [9–10.5 m] deep – and so soft that an iron rod would sink through it. The Railway, for the most part, floats on the surface, being helped by hurdles of brushwood and heather, laid under the wooden sleepers which support the rails. The part of the Moss which gave the most difficulty was about half a mile on the east border where an embankment of about 20 feet [6 m] had to be formed ... Many thousands of cubic yards of stone gradually disappeared before the line of the road came anywhere near the proposed level.

(Henry Booth, *The Liverpool and Manchester Railway*, 1830)

The Rainhill Trials

With the line almost completed, debate centred on the type of engine to be used. Some directors of the company favoured stationary engines, but the Stephensons (Robert Stephenson had joined his father) persuaded them that locomotives should be used. A competition was held to find the best.

Source 5.18   The Competitors at Rainhill, 1829

THE "ROCKET" OF M! ROB! STEPHENSON OF NEWCASTLE.

THE "NOVELTY" OF MESS! BRAITHWAITE & ERRICSSON OF LONDON.

THE "SANSPAREIL" OF M! HACKWORTH OF DARLINGTON.

Source 5.19 The distance to be run was seventy miles [112 km]: and it was a condition, that when fairly started, the Engine should travel on the road at a speed of not less than ten miles [16 km] per hour, drawing after it a weight of 10 tons [10 t] for every ton weight of itself.

On the 8th of October, the *Rocket* weighing 4 tons 5 cwt [4.38 t] including the water in her boiler, started on her journey ... The whole time was under six hours and a half. The speed over the ground, with the prescribed load was frequently eighteen miles [29 km] per hour, and occasionally upwards of twenty [32 km]. The whole performance was considerably greater than required by the terms of the competition, or than had before been accomplished by a Locomotive Engine.

The *Novelty* was the next engine which undertook the appointed task; but owing to some fault with her pipes or machinery was obliged to stop almost at the beginning. Another day was chosen and another derangement took place. Accordingly the owners informed the Judges that they withdrew from the competition ...

From this date, the question between Locomotive and Fixed Engines must be considered as practically settled.

(Booth, *The Liverpool and Manchester Railway*)

Travelling on the new railway

Thomas Creevey MP (1768–1838) travelled along part of the incomplete Liverpool and Manchester line in November 1829. The official opening took place on 15 September 1830, when the Prime Minister, the Duke of Wellington, and William Huskisson, MP for Liverpool, were among the guests on a special excursion. Another guest was a young woman, 21-year-old Frances Kemble.

Source 5.20 *Thomas Creevey's impression*
Today we have had a *lark* of a very high order. Lady Wilton sent over yesterday from Knowsley to say that the Loco Motive machine was to be upon the railway at such a place at 12 o'clock ... and inviting this house to be of the party. I had the satisfaction, for I can't call it *pleasure*, of taking a trip of five miles [8 km] in it, which we did in just a quarter of an hour – that is, 20 miles [32 km] an hour ... But the quickest motion is to me *frightful*: it is really flying, and it is impossible to divest [rid] yourself of the notion of instant death to all upon the least accident happening. It gave me a headache which has not left me yet ... Altogether I am extremely glad indeed to have seen this miracle, and to have travelled in it. Had I thought worst of it than I do, I should have had the curiosity to try it; but, having done so I am quite satisfied with my *first* achievement being my *last*.

(H. Maxwell (ed.), *The Creevey Papers*, 1903)

Source 5.21 *The opening – Frances Kemble's account*
We started on Wednesday last, to the number of about eight hundred people ... The most intense curiosity and excitement prevailed, and, though the weather was uncertain, enormous masses of densely packed people lined the road, shouting and waving hats and handkerchiefs as we flew by them. What with the sight and sound of these cheering multitudes and the tremendous velocity with which we were borne past them, my spirits rose to the true champagne height, and I never enjoyed anything so much as the first hour of our progress. I had been unluckily separated from my mother in the first distribution of places, but by an exchange of seats which she was enabled to make she rejoined me when I was at the height of my ecstasy, which was considerably damped by finding that she was frightened to death ...

(Frances Kemble, *Record of a Girlhood*, from a letter dated 20 September 1830)

Source 5.22 *The opening – death of William Huskisson*
... A man flew by us, calling out through a speaking-trumpet to stop the engine, for that somebody in the directors' carriage had sustained an injury. We were all stopped accordingly, and presently a hundred voices were heard exclaiming that Mr Huskisson was killed ... At last ... I had the following details ...

The engine had stopped to take in a supply of water and several of the gentlemen in the directors' carriage had jumped out to look about them ... an engine on the other line ... was seen coming down upon them like lightning ... poor Mr Huskisson, less active from the effects of age and ill-health ... completely lost his head, looked helplessly to the right and left, and was instantaneously prostrated [knocked down] by the fatal machine, which dashed down like a thunderbolt upon him, and passed over his leg, smashing and mangling it in the most horrible way ... Mr Huskisson was then placed in a carriage ... with his wife ... and the engine, having been detached from the directors' carriage, conveyed them to Manchester.

(Kemble *Record*)

Source 5.23 Poor Huskisson was conveyed from the spot at the astonishing speed of $33\frac{3}{4}$ miles [54 km] an hour, so great was the anxiety of the physicians to get him to the place where amputation (the only chance) could be performed. It was dreadful! Think that out of the hundreds and thousands assembled in the densest masses, he alone should be the sufferer!

(Letter from Currie to Loch, 16 September 1830, Sutherland Collection, Stafford CRO, quoted in Richards, *Leviathan of Wealth*, p. 102)

Source 5.24 Liverpool Station, 1831

_____ **Using the Evidence** _____

1. Study sources 5.7 to 5.10.
   (a) Suggest a reason why source 5.8 may not be a completely reliable source.
   (b) Check the reliability of source 5.8 by studying sources 5.7, 5.9 and 5.10 in
       turn. Find one reason in each of these sources which suggests either that 5.8 *is*
       reliable, or is *not* reliable. Set your answer out like this:
          Source 5.7 suggests that 5.8 is/is not reliable because . . .

2. Use source 5.15 to describe how Olive Mount Cutting was made, and what dangers
   were involved in the work.

3. Look at sources 5.16 and 5.17.
   (a) Use these sources to explain how Chat Moss was crossed.
   (b) How valuable did you find source 5.16?

4. From sources 5.18 and 5.19, write down what you consider to have been the most
   important of the rules of the competition.

5. Look at sources 5.20, 5.21 and 5.22.
   (a) How do you explain the different reaction to their first railway journey of
       Thomas Creevey; Frances Kemble; Frances Kemble's mother?
   (b) Work in pairs: Imagine a conversation between Frances Kemble and her
       mother. They talk first of their impressions of the train journey, and then their
       reaction to the accident to Huskisson.

6. Study source 5.20 again. Thomas Creevey MP had been a strong opponent of the
   Liverpool and Manchester railway during debates in Parliament. How might this
   knowledge alter your answer to 5(a)?

7. Using sources 5.22, 5.23 and 5.24: you are a railway expert, asked to give evidence
   to a fatal accident enquiry. What recommendations would you make, to try to
   prevent a similar accident happening again?

Motivation

1. For this exercise you should divide into groups of four or five. Each group represents a different body of opponents to the Liverpool and Manchester Railway. Each group must use the information to draw up a petition against the railway. Each group's petition should list the reasons why that particular body opposed the railway.
   (a) Group 1 are landowners;
   (b) Group 2 are canal (and turnpike) owners;
   (c) Group 3 are conservationists, who like to protect the countryside;
   (d) Group 4 are sceptics – people who doubt whether an engine or line can be built.
   Refer in particular to sources 5.11 to 5.14.

Similarity/Difference

2. The Rainhill Trials
   (a) What were the chief means of transport before railways?
   (b) What type of engine did some people favour for the new railway?
   (c) How did the 'Rocket' settle the argument?

Railway Expansion

The Liverpool and Manchester proved a great success, and led to the development of many more lines. People everywhere believed there was great profit to be made in buying shares in these new companies. In 1835, and even more so from 1844 to 1846 a railway 'mania' (madness) gripped the country. Vast fortunes were made and lost.

The Stephensons continued to play an important part in these developments, and so, too, did Isambard Kingdom Brunel, who built the Great Western Railway from London to Bristol. Brunel built this track with as few bends as possible, and with gentle gradients, so that high speeds would be possible. As a further aid to safety, he built the line with the rails 7 feet (2.134 m) apart, much wider than the standard 4 feet 8½ inches (1.42 m) which all other lines had in common.

Source 5.25 *The success of the Liverpool and Manchester*
Before the establishment of the Liverpool and Manchester railway, there were twenty-two regular and about seven occasional extra coaches between these places, which, in full, could only carry per day 688 persons. The railway, from its commencement, carried 700 000 persons in eighteen months being an average of 1070 per day. It has not been stopped for a single day. The fare by coach was 10s. [50p] inside and 5s. [25p] outside – by railway it is 5s. inside and 3s. 6d. [17½p] outside. The time occupied in making the journey by coach was four hours – by railway it is one hour and three quarters. All the coaches but one have ceased running . . . the travelling is cheaper, safer, and easier . . . Goods are delivered in Manchester the same day they are received in Liverpool. By canal they were never delivered before the third day . . . The savings to manufacturers in the neighbourhood of Manchester, in the carriage of cotton alone, has been £20 000 per annum . . . Coal pits have been sunk, and manufactories established on the line, giving great employment to the poor. . . It is found advantageous for the carriage of milk and garden produce . . . A great deal of land on the line has been let for garden ground, at increased rents. Residents on the line find the railway a great convenience, by enabling them to attend to their business in Manchester and Liverpool with ease, at little expense . . . The value of land on the line has been considerably enhanced by the operation of the railway . . .

(*Annual Register*, 1832)

Source 5.26 I see *another* Birmingham and Liverpool Road advertised, the whole country will go Rail Road Mad and it will require prompt and decisive conduct on the part of Parliament to prevent the Country looking like a Gridiron.

(Letter from Sandars to Loch, 30 September 1830, Sutherland Collection, Stafford CRO, quoted in Richards, *Leviathan of Wealth*, p. 102)

Source 5.27 *Railway 'Mania' – 1835*
The press supported the mania, the government sanctioned [allowed] it, the people paid for it. Rail-

ways were at once a fashion and a frenzy. England was mapped out for iron roads. The profits and percentages of the Liverpool and Manchester were largely quoted. The prospects and power of the London and Birmingham were as freely prophesied.

(Francis, 1, p. 290)

Source 5.28 *Railway 'Mania' – 1845*
It has been during the last two months that the rage for railroad speculation reached its height ... I met one day in the middle of it the Governor of the Bank at Robarts', who told me that he never remembered in all his experience anything like the present speculation [risky share-buying] ... It is incredible how people have been tempted to speculate; half the fine ladies have been dabbling in stocks, and men the most unlikely have not been able to refrain from gambling in shares, even I myself (though in a very small degree), for the warning voice of the Governor of the Bank has never been out of my ears.

(C. C. F. Greville, *Journal of the Reign of Queen Victoria*, II, p. 34)

Source 5.29 Railway Mileage Open (cumulative)

1831	140 miles	224 km	1847	3945 miles	6 312 km
1835	338	540	1848	5127	8 203
1840	1498	2396	1849	6031	9 650
1845	2441	3905	1850	6621	10 593
1846	3036	4857	1851	6877	11 003

Source 5.30 The Rush at the Door (*Illustrated London News*, 1845)

Source 5.31 The Break of Gauge at Gloucester (*Illustrated London News*, 1846)

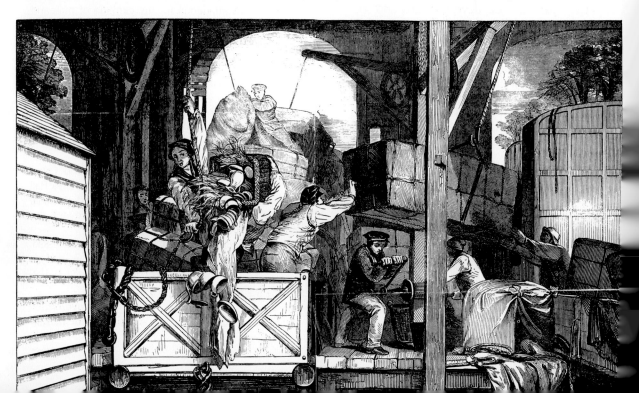

Source 5.32 To the Birmingham Train, (*Illustrated London News* 1846)

_____ **Using the Evidence** _____

1. Using source 5.25, compare road transport with railway between Liverpool and Manchester. Set your answer out in a table like this:

	ROAD	RAILWAY
(i) Number of passengers daily		

2. Look back at source 5.13 on p. 112. How many of the claims in that source are proved right or wrong by Source 5.25? Set your answer out like this:

CLAIM	PROVED?
(i) Vegetation would die	wrong

3. Look at sources 5.26, 5.27, 5.28 and 5.30.
   (a) Explain why the railway 'manias' took place.
   (b) The Board of Trade announced that it would not accept any more Railway plans, for approval by Parliament, for some time after 30 November 1845. How useful is source 5.30 to a historian?

4. Sources 5.31 and 5.32 illustrate the problems caused by the 'battle of the gauges' where Brunel's Broad gauge met the Standard gauge at Gloucester. What do you think was the attitude of the *Illustrated London News* to the problems created?

_____ **Coursework** _____

Using the table in source 5.29 construct a bar graph showing the miles of railway open in 1831, 1835, 1840, 1845 and 1850. With A4 paper, you could use a scale of 1 cm = 300 miles/482 km.

Building the Railways

Although the famous engineers like the Stephensons and Brunel are most remembered, the physical work of building the railway lines was done by groups of man armed only with picks and shovels and gunpowder. They were known as 'navvies' since they had originally dug the canals or 'navigations'. Their lives were extremely hard – an endless round of back-breaking and dangerous work, drink and sleep.

Source 5.33 These banditti, known in some parts of England by the name of 'Navvies' or 'Navigators', and in others by that of 'Bankers', are generally the terror of the surrounding country; they are as completely a class by themselves as the Gipsies. ... their ferocious behaviour can only be equalled by the brutality of their language. It may be truly said, their hand is against every man, and before they have been long located, every man's hand is against them.

(Peter Lecount, *History of the Railway Connecting London and Birmingham*, 1839)

Source 5.34 They were in a state of utter barbarism. They made their homes where they got their work. Some slept in huts constructed of damp turf, cut from the wet grass, too low to stand upright in; while small sticks, covered in straw, served as rafters. Barns were better places than the best railway labourers' dwellings. Others formed a room of stones without mortar, placed thatch or flags across the roof, and took possession of it with their families, often making it a source of profit by lodging as many of their fellow-workers as they could crowd into it. It mattered not to them that the rain beat through the roof, and that the wind swept through the holes. If they caught a fever they died, if they took an infectious complaint they wandered into the open air, spreading the disease wherever they went. ... In such places from nine to fifteen hundred men were crowded for six years. Living like brutes, they were depraved, degraded and reckless. Drunkenness and dissoluteness of morals prevailed. There were many women, but few wives.

(Francis, *History of the English Railway*, II, p. 70–2)

Source 5.35 Making an Embankment, 1883 – 'The Tip'.

Source 5.36 The 'tip' is the place where the material is teemed over to form the embankment. . . Horses were employed to run the separate waggons down to the tip-head ... and sometimes waggon, horse, men and all would go over.

('Report of the Select Committee on Railway Labourers', 1846, evidence of Robert Rawlinson)

Source 5.37 Sometimes, when there was no use for the soil, it had to be lifted up the sloping walls of the cutting and dumped at the sides. This was done by barrow runs, and this 'making the running' was the most spectacular part of navvy work, and one of the most dangerous. The runs were made by laying planks up the side of the cutting, up which barrows were wheeled. The running was performed by the strongest of the men.

(Terry Coleman, *The Railway Navvies*, 1968 Pelican edition, p. 46)

Source 5.38 I went round by Eston. We call it the slaughter-house, you know, because every day nearly there's a accident, and nigh every week, at the farthest, a death. Well, I stood and looked down, and there were the chaps, ever so far below, and the cuttings so narrow. And a lot of stone fell, it was always falling, they were bound to be hurt. There was no room to get away nor mostly no warning. One chap I saw killed while I was there, anyhow he died as soon as they got him home. So, I said, 'Good money's all right, but I'd sooner keep my head on,' so I never asked to be put on, but came away again.

(Elizabeth Garnett, *Our Navvies*, 1885)

Source 5.39 *Navvies' deaths compared with troops in the Napoleonic War*
Thirty-two killed out of such a body of labourers, and one hundred and forty wounded, besides the sick, nearly equal the proportionate casualties of a campaign or a severe battle. The losses in this one work may be stated as more than three per cent of killed, and fourteen per cent wounded. The deaths (according to the official returns) in the four battles, Talavera, Salamanca, Vittoria and Waterloo, were only 2.11 per cent of privates. . .

(Edwin Chadwick *Papers Read Before the Statistical Society of Manchester*, 1846; in Coleman, p. 124)

Source 5.40 Making a cutting, 1883 – 'Making the Running'

Source 5.41 *The* Manchester Guardian's *explanation*
The contractors, being exposed to fierce competition, are tempted to adopt the cheapest method of working, without any close reference to the danger to which the men will be exposed. . . Life is now recklessly sacrificed: needless misery is inflicted; innocent women and children are unnecessarily rendered widows and orphans; and such evils must be not allowed to continue, even though it should be profitable.

(*Manchester Guardian*, 7 March 1846)

Using the Evidence

1. From sources 5.33 and 5.34, quote words or phrases which show what opinion Peter Lecount and John Francis had of the navvies.

2. Using sources 5.35, 5.36, 5.37 and 5.40, describe the method of
   (i) 'The Tip'
   (ii) 'Making the Running', and explain why these were dangerous.

Continuity and Change

1. In sources 5.39 and 5.41, Edwin Chadwick and the *Manchester Guardian* are trying to persuade the government to launch an enquiry into the navvies' dangerous working conditions. You are to write a letter to your MP supporting their campaign. Use all the evidence you can find in sources 5.33 to 5.41 to support your argument.

2. You are an MP who (like 80 other MPs) is also a director of a railway company. You are against the setting up of an enquiry into navvies' working conditions. Explain your reasons in a speech to Parliament. Remember you will have to give some explanations for the high number of casualties among navvies.

The Impact of the Railways

By 1851 the basis of Britain's railway network was complete. All the main centres of population had been joined up, although many branch lines were still to be built. A transport revolution had taken place, and this had affected every aspect of life.

Source 5.42 *The decline of the roads – effects on a coach owner*

Would you state to the Committee whether or not of late years . . . you have experienced any result from the formation of railroads? – I have a reduction on the North road, since the opening of the railroad, of 15 coaches daily.

You are now working two coaches? – Yes, between London and Birmingham.

How many did you work before the railroad opened? – Nine, which I had for the whole year previously . . . what we carry now are mostly people who are timid people, and do not like to go by the railroad. . .

(Select Committee on Turnpike Trusts, 1839, evidence of Edward Sherman)

Source 5.43 *Number of passengers carried by rail, 1842–50*

Year	Passengers (millions)
1842	24.5
1846	43.8
1850	72.9

(From T. R. Gourvish, *Railways and the British Economy 1830–1914* Macmillan – Studies in Economic and Social History, 1980)

Source 5.44 *The Railway Act, 1844*

Be it enacted that . . . all passenger Railway Companies shall by means of one train at the least to travel along their railway from one end to the other of each trunk, branch or junction line belonging to them . . . once at the least on every week day, except Christmas Day and Good Friday (such exception not to extend to Scotland) provide for the conveyance of Third Class passengers to and from the terminal and other ordinary passenger stations of the railway . . .

The carriages in which passengers shall be conveyed by such train shall be provided with seats and shall be protected from the weather. The fare or charge shall not exceed one penny for each mile travelled.

(*Statutes at Large*, vol. XXVI, p. 451)

Source 5.45 Time-Table of the London and South-Western Railway, 1845

ON AND AFTER THE 12TH OF OCTOBER,

The Hours of Departure will be as follows: —

DOWN TRAINS, from Vauxhall.			UP TRAINS, to Vauxhall.	
To Southampton (*Mixed Train*)	8	Morn.	From Southampton (*Mail*)	2
To Woking Common (*do.*)	9 30	"	From Southampton (*Mixed Train*)	6
To Southampton (*First Class Train*)	11	"	From Woking Common (*do.*)	7
To Southampton (*Goods*)	12	"	From Southampton (*Goods*)	10
To Southampton (*Mixed Train*)	1	After.	From Southampton (*First Class*)	11
To Southampton (*First Class*)	3	"	From Woking Common (*Mixed Train*)	12
To Woking Common (*Mixed Train*)	4	"	From Southampton (*do.*)	1
To Southampton (*do.*)	5	"	From Southampton (*First Class*)	3
To Southampton (*Mail*)	8 30	"	From Southampton (*Mixed Train*)	6
To Southampton (*Goods*)	8 45	"	From Southampton (*Goods*)	8

The *First Class Trains* will perform the journey in three hours, taking *First Class Passengers only*, exce accommodation will be afforded for a limited number of Servants in Livery, 13s. each. These Trains will not Stations between London and Woking Common, but will take up and set down Passengers at all the Statior Woking Common and Southampton.

The *Mixed Trains* will call at all the Stations, except the Train which leaves London at 8 o'clock, a.m., whie at any Station, in case Passengers are waiting to go up to the west of Woking Common.

Third Class Passengers will be taken by the Goods' Trains.

SUNDAY TRAINS.

DOWN.			UP.	
To Southampton (*Mixed Train*)	10	Morn.	From Southampton (*Mail*)	2
To Woking Common (*do.*)	10 30	"	From Woking Common (*Mixed Train*)	9
To Southampton (*Goods*)	12	"	From Southampton (*do.*)	10
To Southampton (*Mixed Train*)	5	After.	From Southampton (*Goods*)	10
To Woking Common (*do.*)	7 30	"	From Southampton (*Mixed Train*)	5
To Southampton (*Mail*)	8 30	"	From Woking Common (*do.*)	6
To Southampton (*Goods*)	8 45	"	From Southampton (*Goods*)	8

FARES.

	STATIONS.		FAST TRAIN	MIXED TRAIN		GOODS
Distance.			1st Class.	1st Class.	2nd Class.	3rd C
Miles.			s. d.	s. d.	s. d.	s.
3	London to	Wandsworth	...	1 0	0 6	
6	......	Wimbledon	...	1 6	1 0	
10	......	Kingston	...	2 0	1 6	
13	......	Esher and Hampton Court	...	2 6	1 6	

Source 5.46 Epsom Races – First-, Second- and Third-Class Passengers
(*Illustrated London News*, 1847)

The benefits of cheap travel

Source 5.47 Now, who have specially benefited by this vast invention?

The rich, whose horse and carriages carried them in comfort over the known world? – the middle classes to whom stage coaches and mails were an accessible mode of conveyance? – or the poor, whom the cost of locomotion [travel] condemned often to an almost vegetable existence? Clearly the latter. The rail-road is the Magna Carta [charter] of their freedom. How few among the last generation ever stirred beyond their own village? How few among the present will die without visiting London? ... The number who left Manchester by cheap trips in one week of holiday time last year exceeded 202 000; against 150 000 in 1849, and 116 000 in 1848.

(*Economist*, 1851)

Source 5.48 Excursion to the Great Exhibition, 1851

GT. NORTHERN
RAILWAY.

PETERBORO

OCTOBER.

IN ADDITION TO THE REGULAR

EXCURSION TRAINS

PASSENGERS FOR THE

EXHIBITION

Will be conveyed daily (Sundays excepted) from Peterboro' by the 7.0 a.m. Train, and Back by any Excursion Train. 1st and 2nd Class up to the 20th October, and 3rd Class Passengers up to the 10th October

FARES, UNTIL FURTHER NOTICE.

6s. 5s. 3s.

BY ORDER   SEYMOUR CLARKE, General Manager.

Source 5.49 One of the most prominent social characteristic [fashions] of the present time is the growth and progress of pleasure travelling among the people. The working classes of 30 or even 15 years ago did not know their own country. Very few travelled for pleasure beyond a small circle around the places which they inhabited. But now industrious men of the Midland Counties whose forefathers never saw the sea are able to gain physical as well as mental enjoyment by a view of its mighty waters.

(*Illustrated London News*, 21 September 1850)

Source 5.50 'Pennyworth of Fun' or 'Opening The Oxford Railway'

If you will listen to my song,
I'll not detain you [very] long,
On the first of May the folks did throng,
    To view the Oxford railway.
And to have a ride – [oh] what a treat,
Father, mother, son and daughter,
Along the line like one o'clock,
    By fire, [and] steam and water.

CHORUS

Rifum, tifum, mirth and fun,
Don't you wonder how it is done,
Carriages without horses run,
    On the Hampton and Oxford railway.

From villages and from the towns,
The gents and ladies flocked around,
And music through the air did sound,
    Along the Oxford railway.
There was bakers, butchers nailers too,
Lots of gentlemen in blue,
And all did strive to get a view,
    Along the Oxford railway.

An old woman peeping at the line,
    Said I wouldn't care a farthing,
But they destroyed my cottage fine,
    And cut away my garden,
Where I so many years did dwell,
    Growing lots of cabbages and potatoes,
But worse than all my daughter Nell,
    Went off with the navigators.

In Alcester lives a bonny lass,
    I think they call her Nancy,
Says she, a trip upon the line,
    Greatly would please my fancy,
I will ride by steam, and work by steam,
    By steam I'll on be hurried,
And when I can a husband find
    By steam I will be married.

When the line is finished at both ends,
You may send your cocks and hens,
And go to visit all your friends,
Your ducks and turkeys, pigs and geese,
To any part wherever you please.
You may also send your butter and eggs,
And they can ride who've got no legs,
  By the Hampton and Oxford railway.

A cobbler bold, as I have been told,
  He shouted to his daughter,
Saying, while I put some bristles on,
  And get a tub of water,
Pop on the train as quick as rain,
  And pop away to Worcester
For some soles and upper leather.

And now my song is almost done,
I hope I have offended none,
May they never off the incline run,
  On the Oxford and Hampton Railway.

WILLIAM PRATT, PRINTER, 82, Digbeth, Birmingham.
(From Roy Palmer, *A Ballad History of England*, B. T.
Batsford, 1979, p. 134)

Source 5.51 *The range of goods carried by railways*
In the grey mists of the morning, in the atmosphere of a hundred conflicting smells, and by the light of faintly burning gas, we see a large portion of the supply of the great London markets rapidly disgorged [unloaded] by these night trains: fish, flesh and food, Aylesbury butter and dairy-fed pork, apples, cabbages and cucumbers, alarming supplies of cats' meat, cart loads of water cresses, and we know not what else, for the daily consumption of the metropolis. No sooner do these disappear than at ten minutes' interval arrive other trains with Manchester packs and bales, Liverpool cotton, American provisions, Worcester gloves, Kidderminster carpets, Birmingham and Staffordshire hardware . . . At a later hour of the morning these are followed by other trains with the heaviest class of traffic, stones, bricks, iron girders, iron pipes, ale, . . . coal, hay, straw, grain flour and salt . . .

(*Railway News*, 1864; in G. R. Hawke, *Railways and Economic Growth in England and Wales 1840–1970*, p. 59)

Source 5.52 *Effects on other industries and employment*
The cost of these lines has been £86 000 000 . . . 80 000 000 train miles were run annually on the railways, 5 000 engines and 150 000 vehicles composed the working stock . . . the engines consumed annually 2 000 000 tons of coal . . . 20 000 tons of iron required to be replaced annually; and 26 000 000 sleepers annually perished . . . The postal facilities

afforded by railways were very great. But for their existence Mr Rowland Hill's plan [the Penny Post] could never have been effectively carried out. Railways afforded the means of carrying bulk, which would have been fatal to the old mail coaches . . . The results of railways were astounding. 90 000 men were employed directly and upwards of 40 000 collaterally [indirectly]; 130 000 men with their wives and families, representing a population of 500 000 souls; so that one in fifty of the entire population of the kingdom might be said to be dependent on railways.
(Robert Stephenson, *Address to the Institution of Civil Engineers*, 1856)

Source 5.53 The Electro-magnetic Telegraph at Slough, (*Illustrated London News*, 1845)

Source 5.54 *The growth of towns*
The most important of these changes is the springing up of new towns. On the Birmingham railway, a station was made at Wolverton, about midway from London, the company erecting a refreshment room and a few sheds for their engines. Around these buildings a town has rapidly sprung up, and is so well populated, that the railway directors built a church.

(*Chamber's Journal*, September 1844)

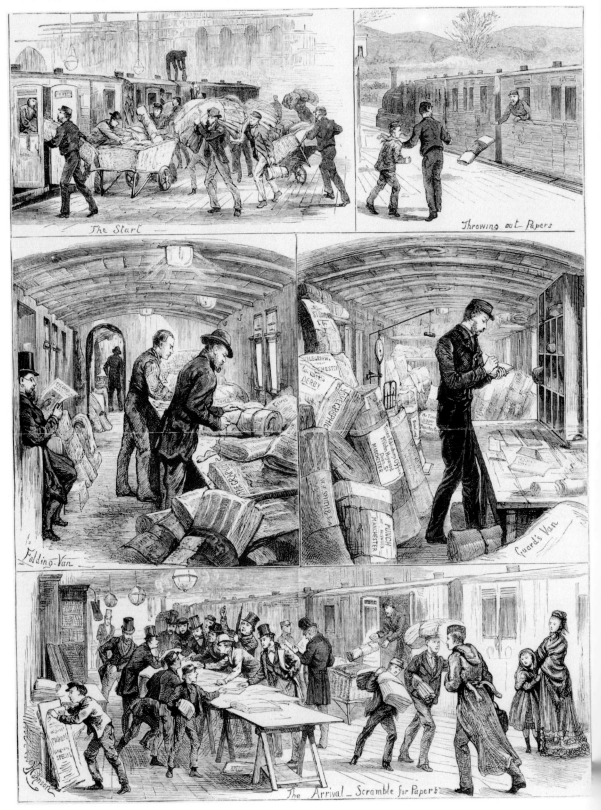

_____ **Using the Evidence** _____

1. Look at source 5.42.
   (a) What effects has the railway had on coach travel?
   (b) Source 5.42 is taken from a Parliamentary enquiry. Think about the people who would be most eager to give evidence to this enquiry. Can we be sure that such evidence will always give an accurate picture of the country as a whole?

2. Look at source 5.43.
   (a) To what extent does this source confirm the evidence in source 5.42?
   (b) Why do you think the figures in source 5.43 only start in 1842? What may be the problem in any such early figures?

3. Look at source 5.44.
   (a) What are the two main terms of the 1844 Railway Act?
   (b) How did the Railway Act make the developments shown in sources 5.47, 5.48 and 5.49 possible?

4. Study sources 5.45 and 5.46 carefully.
   (a) Give examples of evidence from both these sources which suggest that railway companies did not take too much trouble with the third-class passengers.
   (b) How does the artist in source 5.46 show his feelings about the differences between the passengers in the three classes of travel?

5. Using sources 5.51 and 5.52, explain the importance of railways for each of the following:
   (a) fresh goods;
   (b) industrial goods;
   (c) the manufacture of rails and locomotives;
   (d) providing work;
   (e) the Penny Post.

6. Sources 5.53 and 5.55 illustrate two ways, along with the Penny Post, by which railways brought about a revolution in the communication of news.
   (a) 5.55 shows how the famous news agents W. H. Smith built up their empire. Explain how Smiths used both the trains and the stations to help their business.
   (b) Why do you think there was a need for a system like the telegraph to develop alongside the railways?

7. Source 5.54 describes one way in which railways led to the growth of towns. Try and think of other ways in which new towns may have been created, or existing towns enlarged, because of the railways.

_____ **Coursework** _____

Continuity and Change

Source 5.50 was written to celebrate the opening of the Oxford Railway in 1852.
(a) How does the writer show the railway was still regarded as a new thing?
(b) Give examples of the advantages of the railway that he describes.
(c) What bad results does he say it had?

6 Britain and the Great Exhibition, 1851

Iron and Steel (William Bell Scott)

The 'Workshop of the World' – Britain 1851

Britain's industry was developing faster than ever before. People were generally better off than they had been in 1815, although there were still many poor people, as we saw in Chapter 2. British manufacturers exported their products abroad to countries with little industry of their own. To make trade easier, British governments from the 1820s began to reduce, and then abolish customs duties which had limited trade, and persuaded other countries to follow Britain's example. Even the Corn Laws were repealed (abolished) in 1846, despite the opposition of many landowning Members of Parliament. They feared that British farmers would be ruined if cheap foreign corn was allowed into Britain.

Source 6.1 *A German visitor's impressions of British industry in 1851*
I visited England for the first time 52 years ago . . . to judge how far and how completely . . . industrial activity had developed, as against that which the Continent could show; and I must confess that the verdict fell entirely in favour of England . . .

Yet nothing very new could be observed there at that period . . . the same things were to be found elsewhere, though not so good . . .

Twenty years later . . . I found great new developments in the above mentioned field. Spinning mills, foundries, potteries . . . steel and file factories, the plating works of Birmingham and Sheffield, the spinning and weaving mills of Manchester, and the cloth manufacture of Leeds, had acquired a size and perfection of which there can be no conception without actually seeing them.

Twelve or thirteen years later . . . the scale of everything and especially the expansion of London had increased yet more . . .

The already extensive steam navigation, the general installation of gas lighting, Perkins's steam-driven shuttles, Brunel's giant tunnel . . . besides much else of the greatest interest . . . remain in my mind . . . as an ever fascinating picture.

(Johann Conrad Fischer, *Tagebucher (Diary)* 1851)

Source 6.2 *The opinion of Frederick Engels, the socialist writer, on Britain's move towards Free Trade*
Every obstacle was mercilessly removed. The tariff [customs duty] . . . [was] revolutionised. Everything was made subordinate to one end, but that end of utmost importance to the manufacturing capitalist: the cheapening of all raw produce, and especially of the means of living of the working class; the reduction of the cost of raw material, and the keeping down . . . of wages. England was to become the 'workshop of the world'; all other countries were to become for England . . . markets for her manufactured goods, supplying her in return with raw materials and food.

(F. Engels, *The Condition of the Working Class in England*.)

Source 6.3 The British Lion in 1850 or The Effects of Free Trade (*Punch*)

Using the Evidence

1. (a) In source 6.1, how does Fischer say British industry compared with industry on the continent of Europe
   (i) In 1799 ('52 years ago')?
   (ii) In 1819 ('Twenty years later')?
   (iii) In 1831–2 ('Twelve or thirteen years later')?

(b) From the evidence, would you say British industry was
  (i) Developing at the same rate as European industry?
  (ii) Developing faster than European industry?
  (iii) Developing at an ever-increasing rate over European industry?
(c) Fischer was a foreign visitor to Britain. How might this make his comparison of British and European industry a more reliable one?

2. Look at sources 6.2 and 6.3.
  (a) How does the cartoon show that Free Trade was good for Britain?
  (b) Which class of person is shown in the form of the 'British lion'? Is this the same class of person that Engels said Free Trade was intended to benefit? Explain in your own words the difference in point of view about Free Trade in sources 6.2, and 6.3.

For and Against Change

Improvements in British life

There was no doubt that great improvements had taken place in Britain. The 'Industrial Revolution' had made Britain the 'Workshop of the world'. Transport developments such as canals and especially railways (see Chapter 5) had helped the growth of industry. Railways had even made it possible for working people to leave the areas where they lived and worked. More and better food was available because of the improvements in agriculture. The right to vote had been given in 1832 to some of the middle class who were now represented in Parliament (see Chapter 1).

Source 6.4 *The Reverend Sydney Smith noted many improvements.*
It is of some importance at what period a man is born. A young man, alive at this period, hardly knows to what improvements of human life he has been introduced; and I would bring before his notice the following . . . changes which have taken place since I first began to breathe . . . Gas was unknown: I groped about the streets of London in all but the utter darkness of a twinkling oil lamp, under the protection of watchmen . . . and exposed to every species of . . . insult.

I have been nine hours in sailing from Dover to Calais before the invention of steam. It took me nine hours to go from Taunton to Bath, before the invention of rail roads, and I now go in six hours from Taunton to London. In going from Taunton to Bath, I suffered between 10 000 to 12 000 severe contusions [bruises] before stone-breaking Macadam was born.

I can walk, by the assistance of the police, from one end of London to the other, without molestation;

or, if tired, get into a cheap and active cab . . .

. . . The corruptions of Parliament, before Reform, infamous . . . The Poor Laws were gradually sapping the vitals of the country; and, whatever miseries I suffered, I had no post to whisk my complaints for a single penny to the remotest corners of the empire . . .

(*Collected Works of the Reverend Sydney Smith*, Longman 1839, 'Modern Changes')

Criticisms of change

Parliament had passed laws to improve working conditions in factories and mines (see Chapter 3). But these had not gone far enough – hours of work were still very long, and children could still be employed in factories and mines, though not so young as before. Nothing had yet been done to improve safety and health in factories and mines. The Public Health Act of 1848 had set up the Board of Health, but it had been abolished in 1854, and slum living conditions, overcrowding and disease still existed in industrial towns (see Chapter 3.)

Source 6.5 *Fredrick Engels' comments on how the Industrial Revolution affected working people . . .*
In the circumstances [that is, before the Industrial Revolution] the workers enjoyed a comfortable, peaceful existence . . . Their standard of living was much better than that of the factory worker today. They were not forced to work excessive hours . . . eventually machines robbed them of their livelihood and forced them to seek work [in the towns]. The Industrial Revolution . . . turned the workers completely into mere machines and deprived them of the last remnants of independent activity . . .

(Engels, *The Condition of the Working Class in England*)

Source 6.6 Capital and Labour (*Punch*, 1843)

Source 6.7 Over London by rail (Doré)

Using the Evidence

1. Here are some of the improvements noticed by Sydney Smith in the early part of the nineteenth century. Find phrases in source 6.4 to match each of them:
   Faster sea travel   Cheaper than before to look after the poor
   Faster travel on land
   Easier to walk at night in cities   Elections were fairer than before
   Safer to walk at night in cities   The 'Penny Post' had begun.

2. In source 6.5, how does Engels say that the Industrial Revolution had made working people *worse* off than before?

3. Look at source 6.6.
   (a) What was the difference in the lives of the two groups of people – Capital and Labour?
   (b) *Punch* magazine printed this cartoon as a criticism of the richer classes. Using the evidence in the cartoon, say why the rich could live so well.

4. How does source 6.7 show the good and bad results of the Industrial Revolution for Britain?

The Great Exhibition

A Royal Commission was set up to arrange for an international exhibition, which was organised by Queen Victoria's husband, Prince Albert, the Prince Consort. Various schemes for a building to hold the exhibition were rejected as being too large, too heavy or too clumsy. Eventually, a design by Joseph Paxton was accepted. This was for a building of iron and glass. Not surprisingly, *Punch* magazine nicknamed it the 'Crystal Palace'. It contained 1 million square feet (92.900 sq. m) of glass and covered an area of 19 acres (7.7 ha). Yet it only cost £79 800 and it only took seven months to build. Queen Victoria opened the Great Exhibition in Hyde Park, London, on 1 May, 1851.

Source 6.8 *Prince Albert explaining the purpose of the Great Exhibition*
Gentlemen – the Exhibition of 1851 is to give a true test and living picture of the point of development at which the whole of mankind has arrived in this great task, and a new starting-point from which all nations will be able to direct their further exertions.

(From a speech by Prince Albert at a banquet in 1850, in *Principal Speeches and Addresses of H.R.H. the Prince Consort*, 1862, pp. 110–12)

Joseph Paxton explaining his plan for the 'Crystal Palace' to Prince Albert.

Source 6.9 Lifting the transept ribs into place

Source 6.10 The Crystal Palace

Source 6.11 The Times *report of the opening of the Exhibition*

There was yesterday witnessed a sight the like of which has never happened before, and which . . . can never be repeated . . . In a building that could easily have accommodated twice as many, twenty-five thousand persons, so it is computed, were arranged in order round the throne of our SOVEREIGN. Around them, amidst them, and over their heads was displayed all that is useful or beautiful in nature or in art. Above them rose a glittering arch more lofty and spacious than the vaults of even our noblest cathedrals. On either side the vista seemed almost boundless . . . all contributed to an effect so grand and yet so natural, that it hardly seemed to be put together by design, or to be the work of human artificers [workmen].

(*The Times*, 2 May 1851.)

Source 6.12 The Opening Ceremony (Henry C. Selous)

GIVEN BY WARREN W. DE LA RUE ESQ.

Source 6.13 *Lord Palmerston's (who became Prime Minister in 1855) description of the opening of the Exhibition to the British Ambassador in Paris*

. . . Mayne, the head of the police, told me he thought there were about thirty-four thousand in the glass building. The Queen, her husband, her eldest son and daughter, gave themselves in full confidence to this multitude, with no other guard than one of honour, and the accustomed supply of stick-handed constables, to assist the crowd in keeping order amongst them-selves . . .

The royal party were received with continued accla-mation as they passed through the parks and round the Exhibition House; and it was also very interesting to witness the cordial greeting given to the Duke of Wellington . . .

The building itself is far more worth seeing than anything in it, though many of its contents are worthy of admiration . . .

(Letter from Lord Palmerston to Lord Normanby (Ambassador in Paris); in E. Ashley, *Life and Corre-spondence of Lord Palmerston*, Bentley, 1879)

Source 6.14 *Queen Victoria describing the exhibits in the British part of the Exhibition*

Went to the machinery part, where we remained two hours, and which is excessively interesting and instructive . . . What used to be done by hand and used to take months doing is now accomplished in a few instants by the most beautiful machinery. We saw first the cotton machines from Oldham . . . We saw hydraulic machines, pumps, filtering machines of all kinds, machines for purifying sugar – in fact, every conceivable invention. We likewise saw medals made by machinery which not more than fifteen years ago were made by hand, fifty million instead of one million can be supplied in a week now.

(In Eric de Maré, *The Year of the Great Exhibition*, The Folio Society, 1972)

Source 6.15 The Machinery hall at the Great Exhibition

Source 6.16 Part of the foreign exhibits at the Great Exhibition

Source 6.17 *A French visitor comparing the British and foreign exhibits*
While the foreign nave is filled with objects of art, properly speaking, the English is principally occupied with objects of utility [usefulness].

(In de Maré, *The Year of the Great Exhibition*)

Visiting the Great Exhibition

The Exhibition was tremendously popular. A visit to the 'Crystal Palace' was thought of as an important social occasion, and people came from all over Britain to visit it. People from all classes and occupations made the journey. Cheap railway travel allowed many working people to make the journey of their lives to see the Exhibition in London.

Before the famous 'Crystal Palace' was closed to the public in October 1851, over six million people had visited it, and it made a fine profit of £160 000 – a tremendous amount of money at the time. The money was used to buy land on which was built the South Kensington Museums and Colleges.

The 'Crystal Palace' was then taken down and re-built at Sydenham, where it was re-opened in 1854 as a site for all sorts of exhibitions and entertainments. Unfortunately, it was destroyed by fire in November 1936.

Source 6.18 *Lady Charlotte Guest, looking forward to the opening of the Exhibition*
April 30
A large and pleasant party at Lady John Russell's. Everybody was talking about tomorrow's opening. Most people were going, but some few professed to treat it with contempt, and some had not thought it worth while to take season tickets, by which admission could be had. Some days before, a great deal had been said about the dangers attendant on the ceremony. Some affirmed that the whole edifice would tumble down, some that the noise of the cannons would shatter the glass, many that the

crowd and rush at the doors would be intolerable, and not a few expected that riots and rebellions and conspiracies were suddenly to break out . . .

(Earl of Bessborough, *The Diaries of Lady Charlotte Guest* (1833–52), 1950, Chapter XV, pp. 268–71)

Source 6.19   An imaginary picture of London in 1851 (*Punch*, 1850)

Source 6.20   *Preparing to visit the Great Exhibition* Already the working classes in Manchester, Liverpool, Sheffield, Birmingham, the Potteries and the other great iron districts between Glasgow and Airdrie, as well as other places, have commenced laying by their weekly pence to form a fund for visiting London during the Great Exhibition of 1851. Were it not for cheap excursion trains this great source of amusement and instruction would have been unobtainable and the Exhibition would have lost one of its great attractions.

(*Illustrated London News*, 21 September 1850)

Source 6.21   Going to the Great Exhibition

Source 6.22   *The different visitors to the Exhibition* The classes who could afford to pay for their admission having had their turn, from the holders of season tickets, and the more aristocratic and exclusive visitors who love elbow-room in their amusements, down to the five-shilling Saturday people, the half crown Friday people, and the great bulk . . . in somewhat humbler circumstances, who congregate on the shilling days, the turn of those who are too poor to pay for such an amusement has come also . . . the doors of the Crystal Palace have been opened to many thousands of industrious, well-behaved, and admiring people, without cost to themselves . . . Clergymen and landed proprietors in remote rural districts have organised plans by which whole troops of agricultural labourers, with their wives and children, have been enabled to visit London once in their lives, and to see the marvels of art, skill, and industry . . . in a building so novel in its construction, and imposing in appearance . . . Manufacturers in the provincial towns . . . have not only given their workpeople a holiday to enable them to

visit the Exhibition, but have in numerous instances paid the expenses both of the trip and of their admission ... Public companies and schools have done likewise ... We rejoice to see such examples of kind feeling. They tend to obliterate the jealousies, that, to a greater or less extent, exist between the rich and poor.

(*Illustrated London News*, No. 479, vol. xviii, Saturday 28 June 1851)

Source 6.23 The Pound and the Shilling (*Punch*, 1851)

Using the Evidence

1. Using as much of the evidence as you can from sources 6.8 to 6.12, write a description of the 'Crystal Palace'. Mention its size, what it was made of and how it was built, and what people thought of it.

2. What evidence is there in source 6.13 to show that Queen Victoria was thought to be quite safe in such a crowd?

3. Look at sources 6.14 to 6.16.
   (a) Say what difference there was between the goods on display in the British part, and in the foreign part, of the Exhibition.
   (b) What does this tell you about British industry, compared to foreign contries' industry, in 1851?

4. From sources 6.18 and 6.19, say what some people thought (wrongly) might be dangerous about going to the Great Exhibition.

5. How do sources 6.19 and 6.21 show that the Great Exhibition was tremendously popular?

6. From sources 6.20 and 6.22 give as many reasons as you can why working people from all over Britain were able to visit the Great Exhibition in London.

7. How does source 6.23 suggest that the Great Exhibition was something for everyone to enjoy? Who were the 'Pound' and the 'Shilling' in the picture?

Empathy

Imagine you were a working person visiting the Great Exhibition in London in 1851. Use as much of the evidence from all the sources on the Great Exhibition to help you write a description of your visit. Include in your answer:
– how you are able to afford the visit
– where you live and how you travelled to London
– your impressions of the 'Crystal Palace' and the different exhibits in it
– the other people you saw there.

Looking to the Future

The Great Exhibition showed how Britain had changed between 1815 and 1851. Although the Industrial Revolution had begun in the eighteenth century, in 1815, more people in Britain were still employed on the land than in industry. More people still lived in the countryside than in towns and cities. Industrial development had progressed so fast, however, that after 1851, the opposite was true.

The Exhibition also summed up the 'spirit of the age' – the confidence many Victorians had in Britain as the world leader in industry and trade. They were optimistic about the future, seeing almost no limit to progress, thanks to the wealth created by the Industrial Revolution.

Even 20 years before the opening of the Great Exhibition, the famous author, Thomas Macaulay expressed his confidence in Britain's future:

Source 6.24 History is full of the signs of the natural progress of society . . .

If we were to prophecy that in the year 1930 a population of 50 millions better fed, clad, and lodged than the English of our time, will cover these islands . . . that machines constructed on principles as yet undiscovered, will be in every house, that there will be no highways but rail-roads, no travelling but by steam . . . many people would think us insane . . . If any person had told the Parliament . . . in 1720 that . . . the wealth of England would surpass all their wildest dreams . . . London would be twice as large . . . that men would be in the habit of sailing without wind, and would be beginning to ride without horses, our ancestors would have given as much credit to the prediction as they gave to Gulliver's travels. Yet the prediction would have been true.

(T. B. Macaulay, *Critical and Historical Essays*, 1830)

_____ **Using the Evidence** _____

1. In source 6.24, Macaulay was very confident about Britain's future, like many people at the time.
   (a) In his predictions for Britain in 1930, what does he say about
       (i) Britain's population?   (ii) standards of living?
       (iii) people's homes?   (iv) methods of travel?
   (b) Which of these predictions is clearly wrong?
   (c) How did Macaulay suggest that his vision of Britain's future could well be true, even though people then might find it unlikely?

_____ **Coursework** _____

Change

Look back to source 4.3 in Chapter 4. What turning point does source 4.3 show Britain had reached in 1851? How does the Great Exhibition show this? (See also sources 6.1, 6.8, 6.14, 6.15 and 6.17.)

Glossary

Anglican A member of the Church of England.

Borough (spelt 'burgh' in Scotland). A town with special privileges granted to it, usually by Royal Charter. Boroughs had the right to have two MPs. *Rotten boroughs* had few if any people living there, but still had two MPs.

Broadside A song or poem printed on a news-sheet. Broadsides provided working people with information about events and issues of the time.

Census An official survey of the number of people living in a country, and information about them – where they live, their occupations, the size of their families, etc. The first census in Britain was carried out in 1801, and every ten years thereafter.

Chartism A working-class movement whose supporters wanted the *People's Charter* made law. The Charter contained six points which would enable the working class to vote and stand for Parliament.

Clearance Removal of people from their homes. During the Highland Clearances landlords removed the native people so that they could create large sheep-farms.

Commissioner A person appointed by the government to serve on a Royal Commission to investigate, and report on, some matter of public concern; for example, working conditions in mines and factories, living conditions in the industrial towns, the working of the Poor Law and emigration.

Constituency The area an MP represents in Parliament.

Domestic system The manufacture of cloth by hand by villagers at home before the development of factories.

Emancipation Setting people free from some restriction. Thus Catholic Emancipation removed the restrictions which had prevented Catholics from becoming MPs.

Enclosed farms Compact farms of enclosed (hedged and fenced) fields which replaced the old open fields of scattered strips of land in the eighteenth and early nineteenth centuries.

Evangelicals A group in the Church of England whose faith in God made them try to help those in need – the poor, children in factories, etc.

Factory system Mass producing goods in factories, first by water-driven machines, and later by steam-powered machines. It quickly replaced domestic industry in the late eighteenth and early nineteenth centuries – a change referred to as the *Industrial Revolution*.

Franchise The right to vote in elections.

Freehold The right to hold property for life.

Free Trade A system by which countries increased trade amongst themselves by removing customs duties on imported goods. Britain gradually reduced and removed its customs duties from the 1820s, so that it was more or less a Free Trade country by 1850.

Habeas Corpus A law which prevents a person being kept in prison without a trial. It was suspended by the government in 1817 so that Radicals could easily be imprisoned.

Hustings A platform from which candidates for Parliament made speeches and where voters indicated their choice of candidate.

Industrial Revolution The period beginning about the 1770s when factory industry replaced domestic industry.

Laissez-Faire A policy of non-intervention by the government in the freedom of an individual, especially in matters of trade and industry.

Mania A form of madness. In the 1840s people became so over-enthusiastic about building new railway lines and buying shares in railway companies that a 'Railway Mania' developed

Methodist A member of the Methodist church founded by John Wesley in the eighteenth century. Like Evangelicals, Methodists believed in spreading the Christian message to working people and doing good deeds to help the poor.

Migration A movement of people. *Emigrants* are people who leave a country; *immigrants* are people who enter a country.

Navvy A railway labourer. The first navvies worked digging the canals or 'navigations' as they were called.

Nonconformist (Dissenter) A person who belongs to a Protestant church separate from the Church of England.

Philanthropist A person whose love of mankind makes him or her devote a lifetime to helping others.

Radicals People belonging to various groups who wanted far-reaching reforms, in particular, reform of Parliament, so that all adult males could vote.

Self-Help The common belief in the nineteenth century that people should be self-reliant and not look to the government to solve their problems. A famous journalist of the time, Samuel Smiles, wrote a book of this name in 1859.

Suffrage The right to vote. Universal male suffrage means a vote for every adult male.

Tories Members of the Tory (later Conservative) Party, one of the two main political parties in Britain. (The other was the Whigs – see below.) They came from the landowning class and supported the established order, including the Monarch and the Church of England. Most Tories were suspicious of reform.

Whigs Members of the Whig Party, one of the two main political parties in Britain. (The other was the Tories – see above.) They believed in Catholic Emancipation, reform of Parliament and Free Trade.

Bibliography

General

Asa Briggs, *The Age of Improvement 1783–1867*, Longman, 1959
G. D. H. Cole and A. W. Filson, *British Working Class Movements – Select Documents 1789–1875*, Macmillan, 1951
Frederick Engels, *The Condition of the Working Class in England*, 1844, Panther, 1969
Norman Gash, *The Age of Peel*, Edward Arnold, 1968
Norman Gash, *Aristocracy and People – Britain 1815–65* (*New History of England* – 8), Edward Arnold, 1979
Colin McNab and Robert Mackenzie, *From Waterloo to the Great Exhibition – Britain 1815–1851*, Oliver & Boyd, 1982
Anthony Wood, *Nineteenth-Century Britain, 1815–1914*, Longman, 1960

1 The Vote

J. Addy, *Parliamentary Elections and Reform, 1807–1832*, Longman (*Then and There*), 1968
Samuel Bamford, *Passages in the Life of a Radical*, Simpkin, 1844
Asa Briggs (ed.), *Chartist Studies*, Macmillan, 1959
R. G. Gammage, *History of the Chartist Movement*, Newcastle, 1894
J. W. Hunt, *Reaction and Reform 1815–1841*, Collins, 1972
K. H. Randell, *Politics and the People 1835–1850*, Collins, 1972
P. Searby, *The Chartists*, Longman (*Then and There*), 1967
E. P. Thompson, *The Making of the English Working Class*, Penguin, 1968

2 The Poor

J. J. and A. J. Bagley, *The English Poor Law*, MacMillan, 1966
W. Cobbett, *Rural Rides*, Penguin English Library, 1967
C. Dickens, *Oliver Twist*, any edition
S. E. Finer, *The Life and Times of Edwin Chadwick*, Methuen, 1952
P. E. Razzell and R. W. Wainwright (eds), *The Victorian Working Class*, Frank Cass, 1973
P. F. Speed, *Social Problems of the Industrial Revolution*, Ch. 6, Wheaton, 1978
Susan J. Styles, *The Poor Law*, Macmillan, 1985
R. Watson, *Edwin Chadwick: Poor Law and Public Health*, Longman (*Then and There*), 1969

3 Social Problems and Reform

S. E. Finer, *The Life and Times of Edwin Chadwick*,
Methuen, 1952
E. Hodder, *The Life and Work of the Seventh Earl of Shaftesbury*, London, 1887
J. Howard, *The State of the Prisons*, Dent (*Everyman's Library*), 1929
J. Kent, *Elizabeth Fry*, B. T. Batsford Ltd, 1962
Memoir of Elizabeth Fry, 1847
R. Owen, *Observations of the Effect of the Manufacturing System*, 1815
E. R. Pike, *Human Documents of the Industrial Revolution in Britain*, George Allen and Unwin, 1966
P. F. Speed, *Social Problems of the Industrial Revolution*, Wheaton, 1975
P. F. Speed, *Learning and Teaching in Victorian Times*, Longman (*Then and There*), 1964
N. Tonge and M. Quincey, *Cholera and Public Health*, Macmillan 1985
R. Watson, *Edwin Chadwick: Poor Law and Public Health*, Longman (*Then and There*), 1969

4 Emigration

R. Garrett, *The Search for Prosperity – Emigration from Britain 1815–1930*, Wayland, 1973
F. McKichan, *The Highland Clearances*, Longman (*Then and There*), 1977
J. Prebble, *The Highland Clearances*, Secker and Warburg, 1963
P. F. Speed, *The Potato Famine and the Irish Emigrants*, Longman (*Then and There*), 1976
C. Woodham-Smith, *The Great Hunger*, Hamish Hamilton, 1962

5 The Railways

T. Coleman, *The Railway Navvies*, Penguin, 1965
J. Francis, *A History of the English Railway*, Longman, 1851
M. Greenwood, *The Railway Revolution*, Longman (*Then and There*) 1955
L. T. C. Holt, *George and Robert Stephenson*, Longman, 1960
M. C. Reed, *Railways in the Victorian Economy*, David & Charles, Newton Abbot, 1969

6 Britain and the Great Exhibition

The Great Exhibition: A Commemorative Album, H.M.S.O, 1964
Eric de Maré, *The Year of the Great Exhibition*, The Folio Society, 1972
J. B. Priestley, *Victoria's Heyday*, Heinemann, 1972
J. R. C. Yglesias, *London Life and the Great Exhibition*, Longman (*Then and There*), 1970

Index